RETURN TO GREATNESS

RETURN TO GREATNESS

How America Lost Its Sense

of Purpose and What It

Needs to Do to Recover It

ALAN WOLFE

PRINCETON UNIVERSITY PRESS
Princeton & Oxford

Copyright © 2005 by Princeton University Press
Published by Princeton University Press, 41 William Street,
Princeton, New Jersey 08540
In the United Kingdom: Princeton University Press,
3 Market Place, Woodstock, Oxfordshire OX20 1SY

LIBRARY OF CONGRESS CATALOGING-IN-PUBLICATION DATA
Wolfe, Alan, 1942–
Return to greatness : how America lost its sense of purpose and
what it needs to do to recover it / Alan Wolfe—1st ed.
p. cm.
ISBN 0-691-11933-3 (alk. paper)
1. United States—Moral conditions. 2. Civil society—
United States. 3. United States—Foreign relations. I. Title.
HN90.M6W65 2005
306′.0973—dc22   2004024432

British Library Cataloging-in-Publication Data is available

This book has been composed in Adobe Garamond Pro
and Type Embellishment One

Printed on acid-free paper.∞

pupress.princeton.edu

Printed in the United States of America

10 9 8 7 6 5 4 3 2 1

Contents

PREFACE

In 1989 I published *Whose Keeper? Social Science and Moral Obligation*.[1] Western liberal democracies, I argued in that book, suffered from their reliance either on the market, as in the United States, or on the state, as in the Scandinavian countries. To develop a better sense of the obligations citizens owed to each other, both kinds of societies needed to rediscover a third path, one more capable of serving the needs of impersonal strangers than laissez-faire, while also more sensitive to the intimate ties of family and community than the welfare state. Searching for a name to call that third path, I appropriated the term "civil society," then in vogue because of the idealism and courage of revolutionaries in Eastern bloc countries who had found in the concept a way of repudiating communism without turning, at least at first, to the kind of savage free-market capitalism many of them distrusted.

I was by no means the only one to find the idea of civil society, or concepts closely associated with it, attractive. Some third path between capitalism and government motivated Robert Putnam to undertake the research and writing that would result in *Bowling Alone*, his best-selling call for a revival of community in America. Along similar lines, Amitai Etzioni launched his movement called "communitarianism," dedicated to giving responsibilities equal time with rights.[2] It is difficult to convey the sense of excitement associated with what seemed like a major breakthrough in the realm of ideas. Civil society was a concept whose time had come, as citizens in all kinds of societies, including the United States, came to realize that neither the market nor the state, by themselves, was capable of offering even an approximation of the good life.

Whose Keeper? is still a favorite among my books, and I turn back to it frequently. Yet the last couple of times I have picked it up, something seemed not quite right. I tried once, a few years back, to express some of my reservations with the argument I had made,[3] but only after those reflections appeared in print did the real reasons for my dissatisfaction emerge. There were two. One of them was September 11. The other was George W. Bush.

Because September 11 was an attack on the American nation, it served as a reminder to Americans that they actually belong to a nation. By this I do not mean that Americans had suffered from a want of patriotism and that in response to September 11 they began to display the flag, although both of those observations, and especially the latter one, have grains of truth. Instead I mean that a nation is a form of attachment between human beings capable of evoking the deepest feelings of belonging—and expressing the strongest feelings of solidarity. In the modern world, for better or worse, the spirit of the nation takes its reality in the form of the state. When we responded to September 11, we used government to do so. If there was anything lacking in our response, moreover, it is that we did not use government enough, either in our willingness to extend help to the victims of that attack or in our efforts to secure ourselves against future ones. September 11 suggested to me that the third way between the market and the state for which I was searching in the 1980s may be harder to find, and less desirable, if found, than I had once assumed. Attacked as a nation, we ought to have responded as one. Civil society could not have done that.

If September 11 caused me, and nearly everyone I know, to rethink some of their assumptions, no such engagement with received ideas could be detected in the president of the United States. Before September 11, George W. Bush's one big idea was for a tax cut that would disproportionately benefit the rich. After September 11, despite both the obvious need for a collective response and the sense of national solidarity the attack evoked, the president not only insisted on his tax cut, but used every political skill he possessed to get it through Congress. We needed, in the wake of September 11, something tangible to hold us together. Instead we got an economic policy, soon to be followed by a cultural and moral one, that drove us apart.

And that, at least for me, was not the worst of it. In *Whose Keeper?* I had envisioned the market and the state as alternatives, each promising a benefit (freedom in the case of the former, equality with respect to the latter), but both, when taken to their extreme, threatening to become problematic. Combining the ruthless efficiency of the market with the authoritarian tendencies of the state creates a nightmare worse than each by itself can generate, but that was exactly what the Bush administration offered for the United States. Although he spoke the language of a free-market conservative, Mr. Bush was perfectly willing to use government to reinforce the already considerable power big corporations exercised over the American way of life. And although he appealed, as most conservatives do, to libertarianism, he was hardly the friend of civil liberties as he rushed the ill-named Patriot Act through Congress and then argued vociferously for its renewal. If Americans wanted to sacrifice both liberty and equality in order to solidify corporate and governmental power, that, of course, was their choice. But that was rarely how the choice was put. Instead, relying on dubious data and selective rhetoric, the Bush administration did its best to hide its intentions, understanding, by so doing, that if it proudly proclaimed its real goals, it would become even less popular than it was.

When I look back on *Whose Keeper?* its advocacy of civil society, however idealistic, seems too naive and unprepared for the kind of world that produced September 11 and the kind of politics adopted by the Bush administration. As important as community is, our friends and neighbors in civil society cannot defend us against terror. If the state is to be used to support the privileges of corporate power, those committed to a more egalitarian vision of America cannot respond effectively by relying on private charity or nongovernmental organizations to serve the needs of everyone else. The concept of civil society seems crimped and retreatist in the face of the political realities of the day. In arguing for it in the 1980s, I may have been too much of a premature defeatist, backing off from the complexities of the world in an attempt to preserve a kind of ideological purity that I admired then—and still admire today—but now have also come to recognize as insufficient.

Active in leftist circles during the 1960s and 1970s, I moved, as people often do, away from the radicalism of my youth, although, unlike some of my acquaintances during those years, I never moved from the left to the right. Instead I stopped somewhere in the center, probably to the left of center but then again not that far left. The collapse of communism was a major, if not the major, reason for that shift, for although never attracted to the kinds of socialism that existed around the world, I recognized that the United States had been right to show the world that its values— its insistence on liberty and its way of achieving, however imperfectly, democracy—left more good in the world than anything that had happened in Moscow or Havana. In a word, I discovered that my country was one I could admire and respect, and before long, it also became one I loved. When it was attacked, I took to the podium, defending George W. Bush's decision to fight back against the Taliban in Afghanistan and letting my students at Boston College know, in no uncertain terms, that Noam Chomsky and Michael Moore were not going to help them live in a country capable of defending itself against its enemies.

It is difficult for me to recognize the country I love in the Bush administration, given its unfair and disingenuous domestic programs, its ill-considered decision to stop fighting the war on terrorism and to launch the ill-thought-out one on Iraq instead, and its choice of bitterly negative and divisive tactics to secure its hold on a second term. If anything, I see there the kind of political extremism, wishful thinking, misplaced moralism, and dyed-in-the-wool certainty that drove me away from the leftist zealots of the 1960s. Having come to love my country, then experiencing the shock and horror of seeing it attacked, and finally, as if worst of all, watching as the attack became fodder for reelection campaigns and ideological posturing—all this has become almost more than I can take. I am, for better or worse, an intellectual. What do I do about my feelings? I write a book.

RETURN TO GREATNESS

I The Good and the Great

Its military supremacy greater than that of the rest of the world combined, its economy the envy of even its enemies, its culture irresistible, the United States entered the twenty-first century as powerful as any nation in the history of the human race. Powerful did not mean invulnerable, as the world learned on September 11, 2001. But the willingness of George W. Bush to use military force in response to that horror evoked for some the era of Theodore Roosevelt, a president who, as William Kristol and Robert Kagan put it, "implored Americans to look beyond the immediate needs of their daily lives" and, in so doing, "aspired to greatness for America."[1]

Although Kristol and other "national greatness conservatives" originally hoped that Senator John McCain of Arizona would carry out their program of strengthening American power, President Bush's ambitious foreign policy objectives in Afghanistan and especially in Iraq quickly won their support. They were not the only ones who felt that way; former White House speechwriter David Frum and former chairman of the Defense Policy Review Board Richard Perle wrote a book urging Mr. Bush to apply his big stick in places other than Iraq, such as Syria, Lebanon, and North Korea, making, along the way, explicit comparisons between TR and GWB.[2] The president, as it happened, liked the comparison; Mr. Bush keeps a copy of TR's speeches on the coffee table of his ranch in Texas and fills his remarks justifying his foreign policies with Rooseveltian words such as "resolve," "courage," and "sticking the course."[3] Little doubt exists over whom George W. Bush would like to be compared to when historians ultimately make their comparisons.

Theodore Roosevelt was not quite the hero that Americans often make him out to be; ever conscious of his image and his place in history, he stage-managed his claims to greatness as much as he actually accomplished them. Still there is enough achievement in his case—his recognition that regulation of business had become essential; his commitments to a form of meritocracy that, in the context of his time, enabled him to appreciate the contributions of immigrants; his understanding that divisions by class undermined American ideals; his appointment of Gifford Pinchot to manage the nation's forests; and his willingness to use American power on behalf of peace as well as war—that conservatives have reason to identify him in the camp of national greatness.

What is less clear is whether Mr. Bush should be viewed as following in his footsteps. At first glance the comparison seems to make sense: both men were children of the East Coast who discovered their true selves by moving to or spending considerable time in the western portions of the United States; became adults who never tired of demonstrating their masculinity to all and sundry; were not above heaping furious scorn on the enemies each of them all too easily made; showed little hesitation in convincing themselves of the inherent rightness of their views; once in office discovered that people in the countries to which they were so quick to bring the presumed benefits of American power were not, in the end, especially grateful for their actions; and, despite their political achievements, left divisions in the body politic behind them that fueled the wrath of their opponents. As correspondences go in history, this appears to be a fairly close one.

Yet Roosevelt and Bush can be also distinguished in a number of crucially important ways. Appalled by the greed of the wealthy, Roosevelt became an avid reformer willing to use government to create conditions of fairness for all, turning his back on the Republican Party's inclination to reinforce the privileges and power of the already well off. Conservation—today we call it environmentalism—was, as TR once put it, "the great fundamental question of morality,"[4] not a question of increasing the profit incentives for drilling and logging. Roosevelt's vision of war, however imperialistic, included compulsory military service, which President Bush opposes, and the former president, unlike the latter one, put himself all too frequently in harm's way. Roosevelt's allegiance to the Republican Party was always a bit shaky and he bolted from it in the end, while George W. Bush has been among the most partisan Republicans in modern memory. From time to time in the course of his career, TR would look back with a skeptical eye toward some of the imperialistic ambitions he supported earlier in his life, while GWB has shown no propensity to question any of the decisions, but especially the foreign policy decisions, he made during his presidency. We know, in short, that Mr. Bush claimed the mantle of TR, but we have reason to doubt whether TR would be pleased to see his ideas appropriated by Mr. Bush. He would likely admire President Bush's firmness, just as he would be appalled by the fact that Karl Rove, Mr. Bush's closest political advisor, models himself on Mark Hanna, who played the same role for arch Republican William McKinley, hardly TR's favorite politician.

Despite the gulf that separates Theodore Roosevelt from George W. Bush, neoconservative intellectuals were correct to insist that the time had come to take ideas of American greatness seriously; September 11 made clear to the world how central the United States is to its hopes and fears, and after September 11, whether or not one agrees with the decision to go to war in Iraq, the United States has no choice but to engage directly, using military force if need be, enemies prepared to fight a war against it. Like other transformative events in our history such as the American revolution, the firing on Fort Sumter, the 1929 stock market crash, and the attack on Pearl Harbor, September 11 will be remembered as having stimulated a wide-ranging inquiry into the question of whether America's traditional ways of carrying out its public affairs are sufficient for dealing with the new realities imposed upon it. We live in Shakespearian times, in which evil stalks the globe, matters of statecraft, high and low, take center stage, and all too many people die.

Before we can evoke ideas of American greatness, however, we need to ask some questions about it. What exactly is national greatness? Should the United States aspire to it? What are the costs of doing so? Does the fact that George W. Bush's decision to go it alone in Iraq backfired so spectacularly mean that all dreams of a Rooseveltian foreign policy should be discouraged? Can the United States develop an ambitious agenda for reconstructing the world, as at least some contemporary conservatives insist it should, while retreating, as many contemporary conservatives also advocate, from ambition in its domestic life? Conversely, can liberals, generally fearful of war and suspicious of foreign entanglements, be true to their commitments to freedom and equality of opportunity at home if they refrain from fighting for them abroad? If American greatness is so important, why have so many presidents stood for what the decidedly un-Rooseveltian Warren G. Harding called "normalcy"?

Something valuable will have been lost if, having begun to discuss whether America should aspire to greatness, we stopped the discussion because a president who claimed the mantle of Theodore Roosevelt did such an imperfect job of bringing into contemporary politics some of the ideals for which Roosevelt, as well as many other politicians and thinkers in American history, stood. In their fantastically evil way, America's enemies perceive a greatness in America that Americans themselves had somehow overlooked; denouncing us, as the Ayatollah Khomeini so frequently did, as the "great Satan" gets at least half of the equation right. Because of September 11, we now know that we are larger than life to nearly everyone in the world. We have not put the question of American greatness back on the table; it has been put there for us. It is up to us whether we take our country and its potential as seriously as everyone else in the world does.

⌒— If by the phrase American greatness we include patriotic sentiments fashioned for ceremonial events, then all presidents aspire to it. Willing greatness into existence, however, is a far more difficult proposition. It is not the invasion of a small and defenseless country—Ronald Reagan's intervention in Grenada offers perhaps the best example—that contributes to a sense of greatness, for victories achieved in such one-sided fashion seem tawdry in retrospect, even to those who celebrate them at the time they occur. Nor, shifting to domestic concerns, can greatness be given pride of place when a president decides, as Bill Clinton did after the 1994 elections, to substitute for ambitious reforms such small-scale steps as encouraging school uniforms or discouraging teenage smoking, however important each of them may be. Both Reagan's actions and Clinton's were popular, but popular does not mean great. Greatness is made of sterner stuff than successfully facing the exigencies of the electoral cycle. It takes leadership of a particularly tenacious sort to overcome the inclination of entrenched institutions to place self-interest before the common good, the desires of ordinary people not to be disturbed for purposes larger than those of family and friends, the need, on occasion, to disappoint one's closest allies, and the tendency of public officials to find enemies among their immediate competitors rather than among distant threats.

Achieving national greatness involves three tasks: articulating a meaningful vision of the American purpose; assembling the political capacity to transform that vision into reality; and demonstrating a willingness to use force if necessary to protect that vision and that reality from international enemies and, on occasion, to spread it around the world. Oddly enough for a society that so frequently proclaims itself great, all of these requirements have proven difficult to realize throughout the American experience.

When Americans reflect on what their vision of national purpose may be, the two most frequently cited qualities are liberty and equality. Yet there has never been widespread agreement in the United States on what those terms are supposed to mean. Whatever the founders meant by liberty, it obviously did not extend to those held in bondage; if anything, liberty in the first half-century of our existence became the rallying cry of Southern politicians determined to protect their distinct way of life against those who would extend freedom to all. By finally ridding the country of slavery, the Reconstruction amendments opened the door to a recommitment to liberty, but—again this is well-trod territory—American courts were more likely to apply those amendments to freedom of contract than to effective freedom for former slaves and their descendents. So confused remains our understanding of liberty that to this day we are unsure whether, in its name, we are powerless to regulate the influence over politicians sought by wealthy campaign contributors or able to protect children from the handguns easily obtainable by their parents.

Still, there can be no doubt of the importance of liberty to greatness. One can argue, as Americans have throughout the course of their history, whether an unregulated free market best achieves liberty by allowing for an entrepreneurial spirit to flourish or stands in liberty's way by denying to individuals the capacities needed for self-development. Along the same lines, debates have taken place in the United States for longer than a century over whether such liberties as free speech or the right to privacy come at the cost of insufficient appreciation of the needs of national security or of insufficient recognition of one's obligations to others. There are no easy answers to these questions, and we will no doubt continue to be preoccupied with them indefinitely.

The great challenge to liberty in the twentieth century, however, was posed, not by the welfare state, the sexual revolution, or the demands of national security, but from the powerful, if thankfully short-lived, experience of totalitarianism. And that experience teaches that while Adam Smith and John Stuart Mill were correct to insist on the importance of free markets and free speech, Immanuel Kant was even more right to remind us that individuals—their needs, desires, decisions, and actions—cannot serve as means to someone else's ends. Liberty today, much as the American founders suggested in rhetoric if not, alas, always in deed, consists of the idea that human beings come attached with inalienable rights to personhood; to the greatest extent possible, they themselves, and not a coercive force speaking on their behalf, should be in command of their fate. Other societies might be able to achieve greatness without committing themselves to the protection and extension of a concept of human autonomy, both at home and abroad, but the United States cannot. Liberty is too much part of its tradition to be sacrificed for any other objective, and if such personal autonomy is so sacrificed, whatever is achieved as a result cannot be considered great.

At least we talk frequently about liberty, which we do not always do about equality; to take one striking example, the words "all men are created equal" have been cited only twenty-three times by the U.S. Supreme Court in its history, mostly in dissent.[5] Forced to face the issue of equality because of the Civil War, Abraham Lincoln attempted through his magnificent prose to flesh out the promise of equality at which the Declaration of Independence hinted. But as Robert Penn Warren realized when he said that the Confederacy was born on the day Lee handed his sword to Grant at Appomattox,[6] the less attractive meaning of American purpose over which the war was fought—the decidedly inegalitarian one that held that the value of some human lives, based solely on race, was worth less than others—while losing the war, won the peace, and its victory has contributed to a society unwilling to apply the most elementary principals of equality until a century after the fighting stopped. In the aftermath of *Brown v. Board of Education* and the Civil Rights Act of 1964, we speak more, as well as more favorably, about equality than we did a century ago, but our confusion about what it means persists; we cannot decide whether the equality promised by those landmark events mandates that we practice affirmative action or prohibits us from so doing.

Although Americans have disagreed about the meaning of equality, however, they have nonetheless consistently expanded the reach of equality with each passing generation. Individuals denied the most basic of human rights because of their race eventually won their freedom, then their formal right to vote, followed by their actual right to vote, and finally a national commitment to their inclusion in all institutions of importance in American life. Women once denied the suffrage now decide elections. No matter how divided Americans may be over gay marriage, the fact that the discussion is even taking place is remarkable given the fear and loathing not that long ago associated with sex between people of the same gender. American greatness can be neutral with respect to contentious ways of pursuing equality, such as affirmative action or gay marriage; making support for or opposition to such policies a precondition of greatness leads nowhere. But no vision of what the United States should be can be considered great if it carries with it a demand to return to a time when unearned status determined that some would be rewarded more than others. As liberty at its core means protecting an autonomous sphere of private life, equality above all else means denying to no one the capacity to realize their self-chosen goals for reasons so arbitrary that they cannot stand public scrutiny.

Whatever Americans mean by liberty and equality, realizing those ideals in practice has required far more political will than American leaders, hobbled by a habitual fear of concentrated political power, have usually been able to muster. Liberty and equality must exist within the framework of the nation before they can be expanded to the world, but in the United States, the creation of a nation did not come easily. Consider the case of James Madison, the greatest mind among our early nationalists. Madison will always be remembered as one of the two key authors of the *Federalist Papers*, a classic text in the development of the American nation. Yet he also saw fit to author the Virginia Resolution challenging national sovereignty on behalf of the states, and while Madison understood far better than his friend Jefferson the dangers of allowing the states too much room to challenge federal authority, his ambivalence about national sovereignty set the tone for the decades, if not centuries, to follow.

In terms of consistency of nationalist endeavor, Madison must take second place to his fellow Virginian John Marshall, whose audacious U.S. Supreme Court decisions seemed to settle where ultimate authority lay in a society still given to the worship of the local and the immediate. "Marshall," writes the political theorist Robert Faulkner, "was in the long modern tradition of Machiavelli, Hobbes, Locke and their followers in the way he believed one supreme government, state above church, with a superior or sovereign power to command all within its jurisdiction, the primary condition for a proper nation."[7] Even more than in *Marbury v. Madison* and *Gibbons v. Odgen*, Marshall expressed his sweeping view of national sovereignty in *Cohens v. Virginia* (1821). Rejecting a claim by Virginia that its courts were the proper tribunal to hear a case involving the sale of a lottery ticket in the District of Columbia, Marshall held that "the United States form . . . a single nation." "[We] are one people," he continued, whose national existence is defined by a constitution that "is framed for ages to come." State governments have no independent sovereignty; they are instead "constituent parts of the United States" and "members of one great empire—for some purposes sovereign, for some purposes subordinate." When states rights advocates challenged his opinion, Marshall responded in an anonymous pamphlet by asking, "Have we no national existence?" "We were charged by the late emperor of France with having no national character, or actual existence as a nation," he pointed out. "But not even he denied our theoretical or constitutional existence."[8]

Ever the political realist, Marshall understood that local elites, threatened by a distant power they could not control, would use authority close at hand to protect their privileges, even at the cost of weakening the nation, and he would interpret the Constitution in ways that would seriously encumber their ability to do so. Yet Marshall, who lived into the era of Jacksonian democracy, would witness before his death the resurrection of a states' rights philosophy that owed more to the Kentucky and Virginia resolutions than it did to his own majority opinions. A great son of the South, Marshall worried, with considerable justification, that his own region would be the biggest stumbling block to the nation he did so much to bring into existence; as he wrote to Joseph Story in 1831, "I had supposed that north of the Potowmack a firm and solid government competent to the security of rational liberty might be preserved. Even that now seems doubtful. The case of the south seems to me to be desperate. Our opinions are incompatible with a united government even among ourselves. The union has been prolonged thus far by miracles. I fear they cannot continue."[9]

Marshall's insistence that Americans were one people did not imply that those people had the right to choose who governed them; like the other Federalists of his era, Marshall was no democrat. But having put the idea of the nation into play, Marshall introduced, even if against his own instincts, a political dynamic that would lead to the ideal of national citizenship. Federalists were fond of speaking of the need for "energy" in government, but in a democratic rather than aristocratic age that energy could only be furnished by the people themselves in the exercise of their rights, including their right to vote and to participate in the affairs that shaped their common destiny; when the idea of equality meets the drive for national sovereignty, citizenship for all is the inevitable outcome.

Thus it was that Abraham Lincoln took the ideals of American greatness associated with the more high-minded Federalists—as their support for the Alien and Sedition Acts and their threatened attempts at secession suggest, Federalists were quite capable of low-mindedness—and transformed them into a language compatible with democratic realities. No longer were we "the people" of the preamble to the Constitution or even the "union" so eloquently evoked by Daniel Webster; we were now a nation, even, as Lincoln put it, a "new" nation, a word that appears four times in the first four sentences of the Gettysburg Address. Lincoln's vision of American greatness was not without its flaws; if Marshall was no democrat, Lincoln was no civil libertarian. But it is to Lincoln that we owe the idea that a great nation is dependent upon a great people, its greatness lying in its capacity to look beyond recrimination and to redeem itself through ties of mutual obligation. Only after the Civil War did the United States begin to develop the holidays,

monuments, rituals, pledges, and anthems that today symbolize for so many Americans their special sense of themselves as
a united people with a common purpose. Indeed, according to
one study of the language by which Americans describe themselves, it was not until the very end of the nineteenth century
that talk of union faded, to be replaced by an idea of the American nation.[10]

In time, Lincoln's understanding of American greatness
would become as contested as Marshall's, and it would eventually lose out to those as threatened by the idea of national citizenship as John C. Calhoun and other apologists for slavery.
"This is no nation," said Kentucky Senator James B. Beck in
1875,[11] the same year Congress passed its thus far most extensive Civil Rights Act (which would be declared unconstitutional by a very un-Marshall-like Supreme Court that used the
word" nation" only once in its decision, and then in reference
to France).[12] If a nation is defined by the equal right of all its
citizens to vote for those who lead it, surely a minimal definition that implies no commitment to the social rights that twentieth-century societies would later try to implement, Beck was
right; the United States did not achieve formal national citizenship until the Voting Rights Act of 1965 gave the federal government the authority to overrule the determined refusal of
mostly Southern states to allow African Americans to vote.

Divided over the principles America is expected to embody,
and unwilling to establish the instruments of American national government that would enable great leaders to realize
those principles, is it any wonder that the third idea associated
with American greatness—the need to sustain and use sufficient force to defend and extend liberty and equality—has also

been more noteworthy by its absence than by its presence? On occasion, such force will be required at home, as President Eisenhower realized when he dispatched troops to enforce the law upon a reluctant South. But greatness implies as well a willingness to use force in defense of American ideals abroad, and this too has been the exception more than the rule. In the insightful typology developed by Walter Russell Mead, most of our foreign policy actions have been Jeffersonian and Jacksonian in nature, not Hamiltonian or Wilsonian.[13] Rather than viewing the world as ripe for imposition of American principles, we have traditionally suspected the world of wanting to impose its alien principles on us. Our leaders did best when they kept America pure, not when they engaged its power in places we could barely understand. Our isolationists, if that is what they ought to be called, had no problem with the idea of America as a divine nation. But they stopped well short of accepting the idea of America as a great nation, especially if greatness meant, as it nearly always did, higher taxes, compulsory military service, and government-led reform.

There have been exceptions to this distaste for worldwide greatness, none more pronounced than what political scientist Samuel P. Huntington calls the "neo-Hamiltonian compromise" of the late nineteenth century.[14] Men like Alfred Thayer Mahan, Elihu Root, and John Hay believed that they had the opportunity to apply Alexander Hamilton's pro-British, pro-banking, pro-military, pro-interventionist ideals in a way denied to the political theorist who first formulated them. "I am frankly an imperialist, in the sense that I believe that no nation, certainly no great nation, should henceforth maintain the policy of isolation which fitted our early history; above all, should not on that outlived plea refuse to intervene in events obviously thrust upon its conscience," wrote Mahan in 1885.[15] The ideas of the neo-Hamiltonians, like those of Marshall and Lincoln, had their unattractive side; they flirted with racism, expressed contempt for Lincolnesque magnanimity, and, in their zeal to unify the nation, proved themselves intolerant of dissent. Still just as Marshall's national sovereignty led to Lincoln's national citizenship, the latter pointed in the direction of Teddy Roosevelt's great-power diplomacy.

The firmest link between Marshall, Lincoln, and Roosevelt, however, was not their common success but their shared failure. Seemingly entrenched after the quick victory against Spain in 1898, imperialism would be challenged by a resurgence of isolationism in ways strikingly similar to the states' rights revival against Marshall's nationalism and Jim Crow resistance to the Fourteenth Amendment. Empire proved a mixed blessing at best, as Filipino opposition to American troops began a process that would be repeated in Vietnam, Afghanistan, and Iraq. And when, less than twenty years after the Spanish American War, the United States became involved in Europe's affairs, even staunch imperialists like Henry Cabot Lodge found themselves branded isolationists, even if they should be more correctly described, in today's political vocabulary, as unilateralists.

So thoroughly did Americans reject the military preparedness, active government, global consciousness, and high taxes associated with the imperialists that in the single decade after World War I concluded, as historian David Kennedy describes it, "Americans said no to Woodrow Wilson's League of Nations, no to the French security treaty, no to freer trade policies, no to pleas from France and Britain to forgive their wartime loans from the U.S. Treasury, and no to further unlimited immigration from Europe, when Congress passed the highly restrictive immigration quota laws of 1921 and 1924."[16] Due to this reflexlike inclination to say no, Franklin Roosevelt had to take on a struggle against American opposition to foreign entanglements before he could address the struggle in Europe that we now call World War II. Measured against the foreign policy recommendations of George Washington's Farewell Address, Americans, in the wake of two world wars, the Cold War and now the war on terrorism, are more committed to globalism than they have been throughout most of their history. But measured against the even more ambitious plans of the neo-Hamiltonian enthusiasts for American greatness, they have combined their involvement in world affairs with a distinctly American preference for minimalism.

☺— The experiences of thinkers and politicians from Marshall to FDR are by no means irrelevant to early twenty-first century America. A contemporary program designed to ensure greatness for the United States would commit itself to rethinking the meaning of each of the idea's three prongs under contemporary conditions. It would require serious consideration of whether liberty can be maintained and equality advanced at a time of domestic polarization and global instability, along the way uniting Americans around their common hopes rather than dividing them by their economic and cultural fears. Some recognition of the role that institutions, up to and including government, would have to play in strengthening citizenship so that America's collective energy could be rendered as impressive as its individual energies would have to be acknowledged. And any such program would have to be willing to engage the world, using both hard and soft power to fashion an international system in which American values could become a sought-after objective rather than a target for attack. (I will have more to say about these objectives in the final chapter.)

Yet merely to specify what national greatness would require immediately suggests why it would be as difficult to achieve now as it has been throughout America's past. The moment greatness begins to cut deep—when it makes demands on people to change their ways of life, or it asks them to question their rock-ribbed political assumptions, or it requires that they pay the necessary taxes—the number of those who stand for the principle begins to shrink.

To demonstrate that shrinkage, let me be generous and include within the term "American greatness" politicians, visionaries, jurists, and moral leaders willing to subscribe to at least two of its three defining dimensions. Even by this relatively capacious standard, Thomas Jefferson, John Adams, John C. Calhoun, Stephen A. Douglas, Henry David Thoreau, William Graham Sumner, William Jennings Bryan, Mark Twain, William James, Herbert Hoover, Robert A. Taft, Hugo Black, and, to cite a few contemporary examples, Newt Gingrich, Antonin Scalia, Gore Vidal, Patrick Buchanan, and Ralph Nader would *not* be on a list of those who made greatness for America their major priority. Patriotic most of them have been. Thoughtful, sometimes to the point of brilliance, a number of them were. Good citizens, in their own ways, they tried to be. Most of them were more committed to liberty than to equality, even if some of the more contemporary ones reverse the priorities, but very few of them believed in establishing a government with sufficient authority to transform those ideas into reality, and even fewer held that the United States ought to go about reforming the world outside its borders. Uniting them is the fact that each of them valued other goods as much as, if not more than, greatness, whether those goods involved republican ideals of civic virtue, sectional loyalty, unspoiled nature, the voice of the people, economic freedom, effective competition, states' rights, American isolation, civil liberty, the defense of a homogeneous American culture, or world peace. One can be a great American without having stood for the principle of American greatness.

In the other camp, let me include among those who did make greatness their priority Americans who articulated a sense of how nationhood would serve the cause of either liberty or equality (preferably both); who insisted on the national means to achieve it; and who, even if in more isolationist times they blanched at the idea of extending it around the world, at least were cosmopolitan in their recognition that the United States would inevitably become a continental, and after that, a global power. On this list, I would cite as representative examples Alexander Hamilton, James Madison (at least in his more nationalistic moments), John Marshall, Daniel Webster, John Quincy Adams, Abraham Lincoln, Charles Sumner, Walt Whitman, Frederick Douglass, Herbert Croly, Jane Addams, Albert Beveridge, John Marshall Harlan, the two Roosevelts, Walter Reuther, Earl Warren, Lyndon Johnson, Henry "Scoop" Jackson, and, again to mention some living people, Arthur Schlesinger, Jr., John McCain, Wesley Clark, Richard Luger, Joseph Biden, Michael Ignatieff, Michael Walzer, and Diane

Ravitch. In lumping them together, I am by no means implying that all of them were great themselves; even the greatest among them, as I have tried to show, possessed serious blind spots. But they shared the belief that however important virtue or region or free enterprise might be, none of them could be realized outside the framework of a national society strong enough to achieve its objectives.

Greatness, as this exercise in selection is meant to show, cuts across partisan lines: Federalists, Democrats, and Republicans, Northerners as well as Southerners, literary icons, and even fathers and sons can be found on both sides of the greatness divide. Greatness also corresponds with none of the usual political ideologies used to describe American politics; conservatives such as Hamilton and Marshall were for it, while others of a similar persuasion, such as Calhoun, were, at least at crucial moments, against, and much the same is true among liberals, as the differences between, say, a Hubert Humphrey and a Eugene McCarthy (or a Joseph Lieberman and Howard Dean) testify. Indeed, it is not even necessary to be an American to advocate ideas of American greatness; Michael Ignatieff is Canadian. The line dividing those who put greatness first and those who do not suggests a different cleavage than the ones usually advanced to characterize American opinion.

That cleavage can best be characterized as a choice between goodness and greatness. However much they may have differed, and continue to differ today, on what might make America good, members of the goodness camp were (and in the cases of the living ones are) united in their conviction that too strong a government, too ambitious a domestic agenda, and too overreaching a foreign policy will corrupt values that

America has always held dear and that have made Americans exceptional. For believers in American goodness, power is not an end in itself but a means to accomplish an ideal. As a means, moreover, political power is nearly always second best, to be used only when the people fail to achieve the good by their own efforts. Given a choice between being good and being great, America is better off striving for the good. The enemy of the good is not some external force against which it is necessary to mobilize force, moreover, but temptations within the body politic itself, such as the all-too-human tendency to accommodate to the realities of the world as it actually is. To commit to goodness is to strive for perfection and to accept the inevitable disappointment when it cannot be realized. Success is therefore measured, not by such quantifiable outcomes as military power, gross national product, or indicators of equality, but by the intensity and purity of the efforts designed to achieve them. To be good, America, and Americans, must strive to be virtuous; they must cleanse themselves of sin before going out into the world to spread the word—the good news, as evangelicals would put it—of their message. Believers in a good America typically feel that they are on the wrong side of history, but it is precisely their alienation from the way things are going that gives clarity to their principles and determination to their convictions. They need not necessarily be religious—some of them are, in fact, atheists—but they share sincerity and authenticity as qualities for which people and nations ought to stand.

It is not that adherents to the idea of a great America prefer badness to goodness. But they do assign a lower priority to the good just as advocates of a good America assign a lower priority to the great. The great America school believes that no idea, however noble in theory, means much unless sufficient political power is accumulated to realize it in practice, even if the process of making it happen results in compromises that leave the idea less than complete. Yes, power corrupts, adherents to this way of thinking agree, but impotence cripples. Impatient, results-oriented, practical sometimes to the point of cold bloodedness, advocates of American greatness bend principle, and sometimes law and custom, to achieve their goals, anticipating that the relative lack of attention they pay to means will be forgotten when the benefits of their victories are recognized. Corruption is the enemy of goodness, while complacency is the enemy of greatness. Maturity, not perfection, is the achievement advocates for greatness seek. The United States must overcome its sense of itself as special in order to join the real world of nation states responding to pressures within and challenges without. While always threatened from other nation-states that aspire to greatness in their own way, the biggest stumbling block to greatness lies at home in the American passion for goodness.

Not everyone fits within either of these two categories, some because they belong to neither and others because they belong to both. Given the corruption associated with his presidency as well as his manifest lack of political skills, Ulysses S. Grant might be viewed as standing neither for goodness nor for greatness. Progressives such as Louis D. Brandeis and Felix Frankfurter, reformers never quite comfortable with the bigness in government and industry that reform usually implied, understood their task as arguing on behalf of goodness and greatness simultaneously. Perhaps the most interesting Americans never to fit easily into either the goodness or the greatness camps were Woodrow Wilson and Reinhold Niebuhr. Southern, Presbyterian, scholarly, Wilson seems an apt candidate for the camp of goodness, but in both his domestic economic reforms and his leadership during World War I he advanced an ideal of American greatness; indeed, in an 1894 essay published while he was still a professor at Princeton, Wilson offered his own list of candidates for American greatness, including Benjamin Franklin, Robert E. Lee, and Abraham Lincoln, but not Thomas Jefferson.[17] Widely admired as a realist who advocated the use of national power for moral ends, Niebuhr, whose political instincts pushed him toward greatness, like the religious figures with whom he identified, was well aware theologically that too celebratory an attitude toward any one country's power, including his own, bordered on sinfulness, giving him much in common with those who assign priority to the good. Categories such as goodness and greatness can hopefully shed a new and different kind of light on American politics and culture, even if such categories, like all categories, do not illuminate everything.

Of these two visions for America, it is the school of goodness, and not the school of greatness, that has traditionally held the upper hand. Our legacy of republicanism, our distrust of executive power, our fascination with federalism, our fear of standing armies, our commitments to individual freedom, our populistic attraction to direct democracy, our reluctance to involve ourselves in world affairs, our delayed welfare state, and even our inability to abolish first slavery and then segregation (both of which were defended by their sympathizers as not only good, but as the best of human arrangements)—all of these aspects of our history and culture have put those who made greatness first on their political agenda on the defensive. Americans choose goodness over greatness for the same reasons that they prefer to be innocents abroad, to opt for religions that emphasize the purity of the heart, and to insist and to talk so much about virtue and morality. The closer we stick to what we know best, the more likely we will be to resist the temptations put in our path.

One of the most important questions we face as a nation is whether this preference for the good over the great is our best guide to the world revealed to us by the events of September 11. If it is true that the events of that day put the question of greatness on the American table again, whether or not Americans want it put there, the discussion that follows is likely to be greeted with a mixed reception. For some the idea of greatness for America will provoke a feeling of dread, as if this thankfully discredited form of patronizing hubris ought never to be resurrected. For others it will engender a feeling of lost pride, as if the United States needs once again to develop a sense of purpose and the confidence to see it through. Yet neither dread, which would prevent America from using its power, nor pride, which would lead it to use its power unwisely, seem the appropriate ways to think about what this country should be doing. Americans alive today are the beneficiaries of a more than two-century-old struggle between goodness and greatness. At the very least, they need to carry the conversation between them into their own era.

   ⌒— In this book I want to make an argument for American greatness. I recognize that goodness and greatness both have their strengths as well as their weaknesses, and that in the ideal polity, the wisdom of the former will check the excess of the latter. I am also aware that the question of greatness is by no means unique to the United States; Germans once debated the issue of whether their society should be greater or smaller, and in the European Union at the moment, there is an ongoing struggle between those who want to widen it and those who want to deepen it. One falls victim to the seductions of American exceptionalism if one believes that only Americans need concern themselves about how great their society should be.

Still I also believe, and will so argue in what follows, that the United States in recent years has moved too much in the direction of goodness and too far from the idea of greatness. My suggestion that we suffer from a surfeit of goodness should not be taken to mean that we have somehow done too much to make the world a better place; on the contrary, as Graham Greene reminds us in *The Quiet American,* and as our misadventures in Iraq reaffirm, our innocence abroad, once let loose, can be disastrous in its consequences. I am concerned here instead with the price we pay for our conviction that because we know we are good, we need not pay too much attention to how we actually act. When President Bush responded to the abuse carried out by American soldiers at the Abu Ghraib prison in Iraq by saying that Americans do not engage in torture, despite the fact that they so obviously did, he displayed the pathos of America's belief in its own goodness for all the world to see. No doubt the president was convinced of the purity of his, and our, intentions. But a society that prefers an ideal of what it is supposed to be to the reality of what it has become is not a society the rest of the world can trust.

We would be better served by greatness than by goodness because the former is a political and social condition, not, like goodness, a religious or motivational one. In politics, results matter more than intentions. A society in which people have real dignity and respect is better than a society in which people only think they do. A country that is powerful and willing to acknowledge its power is more likely to use its power wisely than one that assumes that what serves its ideals best serves everyone else's ideals. What makes a society great is not proclamations to that effect but a willingness to engage in all the hard work—if not blood, sweat, and tears, then at least the willingness to be taxed and to serve the public interest—a great society entails. Instead of simply asserting its values, a great society tries both to specify what they are and to achieve them. Rather than denigrating the government that serves the nation, it strengthens the one to embody the other. Americans, if the best-seller lists are any indication, want to lead purpose-driven lives, but society as a whole requires a sense of purpose as much as the individuals who compose it. There is something refreshing in the fact that Americans refuse to see themselves as an empire, but also something amiss when they act is if the world around them is barely worthy of their consideration. Putting greatness first does not mean America will become great, but it would better enable us to accomplish our goals as a society—and to be able to face the world with considerably less hypocrisy.

The political work required to make greatness happen is not taking place, at least not in sufficient amounts, in the United States. Neither of our dominant political ideologies, conservatism or liberalism, is comfortable speaking in the language of greatness, although, as I will argue throughout this book, liberals inherited the mantle of greatness from conservatives in the first few decades of the twentieth century and are, at the moment, closer to being in touch with what greatness requires than their ideological antagonists. Were we to commit ourselves to greatness once more, we have an opportunity to get greatness right this time around, if for no other reason than we have not always gotten it right in the past. There will be disagreement, as in a democracy there should be, over which policies ought to be followed if greatness is to be brought more sharply into focus. But our current response to September 11, dominated as it has been by often ugly partisanship and charges of blame, is getting us nowhere; it is, in fact, an insult to those who have lost their lives on that day. If indeed the United States is at war with something called terror, it is time to stop what we almost instinctively seem to do and pause for a big collective breath, stepping back for a moment to remind ourselves of those times in our history when we looked beyond our suspicions and fears to focus with confidence on our hopes and our potential.

II FROM POLITICS TO PHILOSOPHY

As befits a quarrel as long-lasting as the one over whether America should be good or great, each side comes equipped with more than just a set of position papers dealing with the issues of the day; who can recall on which side of the free trade issue stood Alexander Hamilton? (He was for the most part a protectionist, although later-day Hamiltonians would prove to be free-traders.) Before we can understand why thinkers or leaders took the positions they did on antitrust legislation or immigration reform, it is necessary to consider how they understood human beings and their place in the world. Are people inherently sinful and in need of firm guidance or capable of an inherent moral goodness? Should they be allowed the freedom to discover what is in their own self-interest or ought their actions be channeled toward pre-chosen ends? Are we best off learning from experience or ought we to follow the dictates of logic and theory? Is the world in which we find ourselves the proper world for judging our actions or can we envision other worlds to which we should aspire? Is the present determined by the past or can one escape the dictates of history? Is realpolitik or idealism the best guide for political action?

Goodness and greatness each have their characteristic take on these enduring theological and philosophical questions. Examining how we have approached them is a fitting starting point for an inquiry into American greatness. Doing so we can learn that the choice between goodness and greatness has been with us since our society began, and that, while the contest between them has been intense, we have consistently chosen the goal of being good over the prospect of being great. At the same time, knowing more about what goodness and greatness demand of people and their government, we can also begin to understand what greatness might mean under early twenty-first-century conditions, as well as to ponder which contemporary political ideology and set of leaders is best able to bring it back into being.

◠— One of the most striking contrasts between America's two visions of itself involves something closer to a psychological disposition than a political platform. Nations, as well as the people who embody them, can approach the world with suspicion and distrust or with confidence and enthusiasm. Advocates of goodness lean toward the pessimistic side concerning human purpose, while enthusiasts for greatness can invariably be found on the positive side.

Of these two dispositions, it has been the warier one that has dominated American political culture since the time of the Revolution. It was not merely that the leaders of the American colonies had come to distrust Great Britain as they formulated the ideas and actions that would lead to the American revolution. Their distrust extended specifically to one faction within Britain, those identified, not with the Country, but with the Court. As we know from the work of Gordon Wood, Bernard Bailyn, and other historians more interested in ideas than interests, the Court favored a politics of patronage and mutual back-scratching among men of influence and standing, while the Country spoke of the need for an administrative apparatus that was free of corruption, open to men of talents, and parsimonious.[1] Convinced that the insidious machinations of Court insiders gave them influence out of proportion to either their numbers or the merits, American revolutionaries were inclined to what later generations of academics would call a hermeneutics of suspicion. Europe, aristocracy, cities—these were bad. The colonies, agriculture, democracy—these were good. Were America to make the mistake of pursuing greatness, it would fall into the European trap, a fate against which there could never be too many warnings. Heeding those warning, the Country persuasion, as it has been described by Stanley Elkins and Eric McKitrick was "an ideology of suspicion and resistance, tough and serviceable for purposes of revolution, though less of an asset when it came to nation-building."[2]

Nation-building would be on the agenda the moment the revolution was over, yet this legacy of distrust—the sense that politics is always in control of people whose motives are murky and whose designs are ominous—has been a marked feature of American political culture ever since. (To cite just one example, David Riesman's distinction between the "moralizer" and "inside dopster" styles of political character from his 1950 book *The Lonely Crowd* corresponds almost exactly to the Court-Country antagonisms of the eighteenth century.)[3] In its extreme form—for example among those citizens of Ashfield, Massachusetts, who, in the aftermath of the Revolution, wanted to be governed by no one but God—suspicion could be paralyzing, at least as far as efforts to promote collective action in the here-and-now are concerned. And even when early Americans were willing to acknowledge the necessity of government, their suspicious disposition led them to encumber it with as many constraints as they could envision. "If the persons to whom the trust of government is committed hold their places for short terms; if they are chosen by the unbiased voices of a majority of the states, and subject to their instruction; Liberty will be enjoyed in its highest degree," wrote Richard Price in 1776, sounding exactly like a Republican Party signatory to the Contract with America more than two hundred years later. "But if they are chosen for long terms by a part only of the state; and if during that term they are subject to no controul from their constituents; the very idea of Liberty will be lost, and the power of chusing constituents becomes nothing but a power, lodged in a *few*, to chuse at certain periods, a body of *Masters* for themselves and for the rest of the Community."[4] A people as persuaded of the power of goodness as the Americans should avoid as much as possible making a pact with that particular devil called government.

From the Revolution through the America of today, suspicion has been the most visible feature of those who insisted on the priority of goodness over greatness. Andrew Jackson, a strong president who enhanced executive power but was also a determined opponent of the quintessentially Hamiltonian venture of a national bank, made suspicion into a political art form. Andrew Johnson, who did so much to unravel Lincoln's steps toward one nation, was, according to Senator John Sherman of Ohio, "suspicious of everyone,"[5] and, as his biographer wrote, he "brooded over the wrongs, real and imaginary, which were thoughtlessly foisted upon him by his social betters, and

out of his inner world of suspicious fantasy he evolved an ex-
travagant credo of plebeian democracy and honest toil."[6] Populism has been described by its leading contemporary historian
as "proudly defensive" and engaged in "nurturing a language
of bitterness and betrayal."[7] In terms of their willingness to use
American power abroad, isolationists differ from unilateralists,
since the former generally oppose foreign adventures while the
latter want to undertake them alone, yet both are inclined to
be suspicious of any country that is not the United States. Free
market advocates are suspicious of government. Ecologists suspect corporations and their designs on the earth. Advocates of
term limits suspect politicians. Politicians in the Senate, honoring the tradition of separation of powers, tend to be wary
of those in the House. America's political culture sometimes
appears extraordinarily fractured, but uniting nearly everyone
is a distrust of everyone else.

Sustaining this sense of wariness toward power and purpose
is the underlying conviction, shared by nearly all advocates for
American goodness, that human nature is deeply flawed. Reading through the literature of the anti-Federalists, Cecelia Kenyon found references to " 'the natural lust of power so inherent
in man'; to 'the predominant thirst of domination which has
invariably and uniformly prompted rulers to abuse their
power'; to 'the ambition of man, and his lust for domination';
to rulers who would be 'men of like passions,' having 'the same
spontaneous inherent thirst for power with ourselves.' "[8] Such
eighteenth-century language would have seemed quite familiar
to many a nineteenth-century clergyman. One of them, Lyman
Beecher, wrote in "The Perils of Atheism" of human beings
who behaved like "famished, infuriated animals, goaded by in-

stinct and unrestrained by protective hopes and fears." For men like Beecher, the true theorist of the state of nature was neither Locke nor Hobbes but Calvin; if a capricious God was capable of doing little to transform the human propensity to sin, then surely government could do even less. Beecher himself was a Whig, and for that reason, for all his skepticism toward the human condition, he actually belonged to the more optimistic party of his time. Democrats, the other party of the first half of the nineteenth century, were even more persuaded than Beecher of the darkness of human nature. As historian Daniel Walker Howe writes, these Democrats tended to be Old School Presbyterians holding to a theology that can be described as political premillennialism.[9] For them, more confessional and doctrinally orthodox than their New School antagonists, life on this earth was filled with suffering and sin, and Christ would be required to make his appearance before the millennium to show human beings the errors of their ways.

Those anxious to build a nation and then to make it great have typically had little truck with such splashing around in dark waters. To advocate greatness, their first task was to confront all this talk of how human beings were crimped and constrained by their sinful and ugly instincts. "If all men were angels," Madison famously wrote, "no government would be necessary." But not being angels, it did not follow that they were devils; in a lesser known sentence from the *Federalist Papers*, Madison also wrote that "As there is a degree of depravity in mankind which requires a certain degree of circumspection and distrust, so there are other qualities in human nature which justify a certain portion of esteem and confidence."[10] Madison's coauthor Hamilton, as Cecelia Kenyon points out, was frequently charged by his critics as being far too optimistic about human nature, as, indeed, he was. To create a new society, after all, Hamiltonians recognized the need for government to have sufficient capacity to exercise power, and that in itself, for an anti-Federalist, was a sure sign of hopeless naïveté. "Sir," as Hamilton put it when he addressed the New York State Ratifying Convention in June 1788, "when you have divided and nicely balanced the departments of government; when you have strongly connected the virtue of your rulers with their interest; when, in short, you have rendered your system as perfect as human forms can be—you must place confidence; you must give power."[11]

Many Whigs—Lyman Beecher is the exception here—inherited from Hamilton this sense of human and social potentiality, none more so than economist Henry Carey, a convert from his famous father Mathew's Catholicism, who developed a program of internal improvement and protective tariffs that, in his view, would bring together American social classes in ways that would enable them to recognize their common interests. The Whig Party—and to a significant degree the Republican Party that followed it—was committed to a political theology of postmillennialism, to cite again Howe's terminology. Human beings might be sinful, but they did have considerable control over their fate; their capacity to improve their condition in this world convinced many an antislavery evangelical in the nineteenth century that, as Lincoln would famously put it, there were "better angels" in our nature and, as a result, an apocalyptic doom was not necessarily our fate.

This confidence in human beings and the institutions they created easily survived the Civil War. In perhaps the most famous effort to revive Hamilton for a different world, Herbert

Croly spoke glowingly of the "promise" of American life. Jefferson, he wrote with some dismay, "believed theoretically in human goodness, but in actual practice his faith in human nature was exceedingly restricted." Croly would have nothing to do with such restrictions. A great admirer of Theodore Roosevelt, Croly argued that anyone committed to what he called "a democracy of suspicious discontent, of selfish claims, of factious agitation, and of individual and class aggression" should properly distrust TR's program, for Roosevelt, in his view, was committed to a "salutary and formative democratic purpose" designed "for the joint benefit of individual distinction and social improvement."[12] There is a direct line from Carey to Croly, and what connects the two points is the indissoluble link between the idea of a strong and powerful society and the assumption of a beneficent human nature.

Croly was a Progressive, and of all the political movements that have come and gone in America, the Progressives come closet to combining goodness and greatness in one, often contradictory, mixture; when Progressives spoke, it was often difficult to determine whether their language was religious in its quest for redemption or political in its demands for reform.[13] Still, there is no doubting the sheer scope of their ambition. Reform, as a Methodist minister from Indiana put it with considerably immodesty in 1901, had to be brought "to the home, to social customs, to the organization of industries, to education, to government, to diplomacy, to literature and the fine arts, to the correction of social evils, etc., as well as to the eternal welfare of human hearts."[14] To these tasks progressives brought a Chautauqua-like optimism that bothered some Americans of the time, such as William James, who found the

Progressive sense of uplift depressing. But their zeal could be contagious. Progressives, as the historian Michael McGerr argues, aimed at nothing less than a reworking of people, the state that governed them, and all organizations and associations in between. Indeed, as McGerr concludes, their commitment to reform was so grand in scope and so demanding of people's energies and commitments that Progressivism would ultimately not only fail, but leave a suspicion about the achievement of great objectives that would remain part of American political culture until the present time.

It is not widely remembered, except among historians, that the Progressives had their doubts about Franklin Delano Roosevelt, viewing him as going too far in some areas, such as his reliance on government, while not going far enough in others, especially his lack of interest in the moral reforms that progressives had considered so much part of their agenda. Still, FDR shared with the progressives, and especially with his cousin Theodore, an overwhelming sense of confidence in himself and his ideas. As all politicians are wont to do, both Roosevelts at times would focus on the devious designs of their enemies, but the brooding suspicion of human nature and human institutions so pervasive in American political culture made little headway into either of their administrations. Each Roosevelt in his own way was attracted to what later would come to be called "the power of positive thinking," a term that would almost immediately come to be derided by critics for its intellectual shallowness, but which nonetheless had strong resonance among Americans looking for greatness in their leaders.

Indeed one of the fascinating questions raised by the contagious optimism of the two Roosevelts is why so few of the politicians that came after them embodied it. One can find, to be sure, similar dispositions in the presidencies of John F. Kennedy and Ronald Reagan, both of whom lacked the grand visions of the Roosevelts, even if they shared their sense that the United States needed to break its habitual attitude of suspicion toward human purpose. Yet a striking number of contemporary presidents chose not to emulate their self-confidence; to cite just two examples, Republican Richard Nixon was a brooding twentieth-century clone of Andrew Johnson, and Democrat Jimmy Carter, an evangelical preoccupied with sin, offered, like antebellum Democrats, little in the way of inspiration and promise. However necessary sunny optimism may be for long-term political success, dour pessimism is so rooted in American political culture that it is not easily abandoned. We may think of ourselves as great, but we instinctively reach for the good, and when we do, we allow our conviction that human beings are inherently flawed to trump our hope that they are capable of great acts—and then we elect our presidents accordingly.

ᐱ— Besides attitudes toward human nature, visions of a good America and those of a great America correlate with the ways in which political movements think about rules, systems, and principles. If human beings are corrupt and sinful, and the institutions they create sufficiently imperfect to warrant constant suspicion, then at the very least society requires some other mechanism for ensuring the maintenance of order. Those who take a darker view of human nature often find reassurance in systems, whether embedded in systematic theology, constitutional texts literally applied, economic theory, or a complex utilitarian calculus, through which instincts can be tamed, disobedience punished, and goodness rewarded. Perhaps America's greatest systematizer was John C. Calhoun, who invented an entire political theory and constitutional order designed to ensure that the national government would never develop sufficient authority to impose its will on the states. Far more than the Constitution itself, Calhoun's notion of "concurrent majorities" represented an effort to tame the passions through procedures, as if legal abstractions could be put in place of real people. Say what you will about Calhoun's apologies for slavery, he was at heart a man who stood on principle; as Calhoun wrote in a letter to Bolling Hall in 1831, "I would do anything for Union, except to surrender my principles."[15]

Later defenders of Calhoun's beloved South would share his intellectual sensibilities; whatever Andrew Johnson's strengths and weaknesses, Eric McKitrick has written, "he was no experimenter." In words that could apply exactly to Calhoun, McKitrick points out that "the texture of Johnson's mind was essentially abstract. Concrete problems never had the power to engage his interest that 'principles' had; the principles of equal rights, local self-rule, states' rights as well as Union, and strict constitutionalism had served him through all vicissitudes and had taken on mystic powers with the passage of the years."[16] Consistently enough, twentieth-century defenders of states' rights, such as those affiliated with the Federalist Society, would manifest much the same quality of mind shown by Calhoun and Johnson, insisting that fixed principles established in the eighteenth century prevented government from responding according to the wishes of majorities in the twenty-first. Running through the minds of all these theorists is the conviction that bad people—those who are power hungry, ambitious, worldly, corrupt—threaten the existence of a good society. The only way to prevent them from destroying it is to establish timeless rules with which no human beings can tamper.

For advocates of American greatness, by contrast, principles may count for something, but experience counts for more. We need not fear opening ourselves to the uncertainties of experience, Hamilton believed, precisely because we need not fear human nature. The "supposition of universal venality in human nature," he wrote in *Federalist 76*, "is little less an error in political reasoning, than the supposition of universal rectitude. The institution of delegated power implies, that there is a portion of virtue and honor among mankind, which may be a reasonable foundation of confidence. And experience justifies the theory."[17] Hamilton could not be familiar with the term "self-fulfilling prophecy," a twentieth-century expression. But he understood well enough the logic behind it; insist that human beings require firm adherence to principle because they are flawed, and they will act flawed and therefore require fixed adherence to principle. Trust them and their instincts, and they are capable of surprise.

If Hamilton opened himself to experience, Lincoln had experience forced upon him. Reverent toward the Constitution and the principles it established, Lincoln was not above bending the meaning of the Constitution as a way to save the nation. Indeed some scholars, such as Daniel Lazare and George Fletcher, claim that Lincoln essentially invented a second— or, in Fletcher's account, a "secret"—constitution that made national unity, and not a set of flawed agreements hammered out in a previous century, the basis of American law. That may be an extreme interpretation of what happened to the United States during the Civil War, but there is no doubt that Lincoln was quite aware of Calhoun's tenacious commitment to principle and realized that adhering to it would split the country in two. In that sense Fletcher is correct that under Lincoln's leadership, we "abandoned the language of the late eighteenth century, the language of the documents drafted in Philadelphia in 1776 and 1787, and [had] begun to think of ourselves as a nation with a distinctive historical personality."[18]

Experimentation was also on strong display among those twentieth-century reformers who insisted that the principles supposedly embodied for all time in the Constitution did not prevent government from correcting the ills of a laissez-faire economy. Long before he became a U.S. Supreme Court justice critical of doctrinaire interpretations of laissez-faire, Oliver Wendell Holmes wrote the most famous sentence ever written by an American lawyer: "The life of the law has not been logic; it has been experience."[19] Like the pragmatist philosophers who joined him, however briefly, in the now famous Metaphysical Club,[20] Holmes distrusted absolutes. Translated into jurisprudence by lawyers and judges influenced by Holmes, this preference for experience over theory came to be called legal realism, which was committed to two kinds of skepticism, one toward rules and the other toward facts.[21] The former led realists to the conclusion that there was no procedure for algorithmically applying a preordained rule to any particular circumstance because, in reality, the choice facing a judge was which of many rules ought to be applied to circumstances that cannot be defined with exactitude. And the latter led realists to rely—naively, one wants to say in retrospect—on social science findings in order to adjudicate for the world that actually existed.

American legal realism reached its peak of influence in the period between the two world wars, and its most lasting legacy was to furnish the tools by which the administrative and political innovations of the New Deal could pass constitutional muster.[22] Its skepticism toward rules and facts permitted legal realism to overcome the habitual American skepticism of motives, thereby allowing the nation-state to look beyond the ideological strictures of laissez-faire in order to allow confidence in government. No wonder that New Deal jurisprudence, like Lincoln's, essentially rewrote the Constitution, as Bruce Ackerman has argued at considerable length; even while professing adherence to Constitutional principles, judges who insisted on greatness rewrote those principles to account for new realities, amending the Constitution informally without relying on the cumbersome amendment process.[23]

It is fitting that the New Deal witnessed the triumph of a legal theory that had originated in American pragmatism, since Roosevelt himself was such a tinkerer in the realm of public policy. Like strict constructionists of the Constitution, economists tended to be wedded to abstract theoretical propositions hard-wired into human nature. During the 1930s, one of the most firmly held of those theoretical principles held tenaciously to the ideas behind the gold standard, which dictated that domestic economies reduce their public spending in order to maintain a balance-of-payments equilibrium. Now that we are no longer under the spell of this rather arcane theory—Richard Nixon formally took us off the gold standard in 1971—we are apt to forget how inexorable its laws were held to be; had

Roosevelt been a believer in systems and principles, he would have taken steps to further deflate an economy already suffering from severe deflation. This, as we know, he did not do; the New Deal was a decisive break with the idea that political actions had to be constrained by theoretical demands and instead gave voice to the idea, so prominent in Hamilton's *Federalist* reflections, that experience could be substituted in its place. "We could throw out pieces of theory," Rexford Tugwell would later say, "we could suggest relations; and perhaps the inventiveness of the suggestion would attract his notice. But the tapestry of the policy he was weaving was guided by an artist's conception which was not made known to us." Other New Dealers were equally impressed by Roosevelt's pragmatic reliance on experience. "What are you going to say when they ask you the political philosophy behind TVA?" Progressive Senator George Norris once asked Roosevelt. "I'll tell them it's neither fish nor fowl," was Roosevelt's reply, "but, whatever it is, it will taste awfully good to the people of the Tennessee Valley."[24]

The great fear motivating those who commit themselves to principle is that experience offers an untrustworthy guide. Once untethered from widely accepted precepts, there will, in their view, be nothing left in place to prevent us from sliding into expediency, in the extreme case sacrificing our commitments to democracy—the very definition of goodness itself—for the sake of something that may, but most likely will not, relieve our present discontents. Yet strict adherence to principle can lead us to tie our hands even before events in the world tie them for us. We must, from the perspective of those who opt for greatness over goodness, be prepared to act as new conditions demand; if there is danger everywhere in the world, we should gamble with making wrong choices before we risk doing nothing. Aspirants for American greatness did indeed make a number of wrong choices, including Lincoln's weakness for bad generals and FDR's decision to try to pack the U. S. Supreme Court. But without their willingness to make the big choice for experience over principle, the crises they faced were far less likely to have been resolved in ways that allowed the American nation to continue.

⌐⌐ These differences over the relative weight to be assigned to theory rather than experience have been reinforced by what can only be called the artistic sensibilities of varying approaches to American purpose. Hard-bitten, suspicious, and abstract, it is difficult to imagine advocates of American goodness as romantics, but in the atmosphere of the mid–nineteenth-century, their outlook on the world nonetheless had much in common with the rebelliousness of those literary and musical figures who found in emotions and feelings a more authentic voice than reason could provide.

Andrew Jackson—whose Tennessee roots conveyed the picaresque exploits of Daniel Boone as well as the chivalric code of the South, whose military career seemed to demonstrate the purifying potential of violence, and whose personal code of conduct gave pride of place to honor and loyalty—was in many ways the great romantic hero of American politics. As nineteenth-century artists found their materials in popular legends and indigenous music, Jackson helped formulate, and then came to symbolize, America's first viable folk tradition.[25] His nationalism, a rebellion against aristocratic refinement

and artificiality symbolized by the European court, was never short on patriotism, but the folk community for which he stood also had little in common with the idea of American greatness. Great societies—cosmopolitan, polyglot, multilingual, syncretic—come far too close to the aristocratic societies romantics despise. Folk communities, by contrast, are pure, innocent, and homogeneous; like empires, they give pride of place to military valor, but more for the protection of honor than for the incorporation of the distant and the strange. Jackson's quasi-Rousseauesque vision of a good society has been well described by his most recent biographer: "He had a conception of civilization that placed the idealized 'American people' at a deliberately chosen place on nature's spectrum between 'opulent' city dwellers (divorced from, and thus unproven in, the natural realm) and the uncivilized, morally unfit Indian 'barbarian.' "[26]

The political scientist who best understands the romantic instincts of American political culture is Samuel Huntington, who calls attention to those periods of American history dominated by what he calls "creedal passion." Such periods, he writes, are "distinguished by widespread and intense moral indignation. Political passions are high, existing structures of authority are called into question, democratic and egalitarian impulses are renewed, and political change—anticipated and unanticipated—occurs."[27] The romantic temperament so visibly on display during such periods is deeply moral, or, more properly, moralistic. Good and evil are sharply distinguished in the black-and-white mind of the romantic, and evil, when found, must be destroyed root and branch. (Jackson lacked the scholarly eloquence of so many of the founders, but, as Andrew

Burstein writes, "this lack also attracted many people who respected a clear-cut, no-nonsense man with undisguised purposes.")[28] Passion itself is much preferred to matter-of-fact analysis and clinical detachment. The romantic is more interested in making society authentic—more organic, simpler, in touch with the verities of yesterday—than in rendering it great. The primary task is to attend to the sick souls of individuals, and only secondarily to engage in extensive, and usually futile, efforts at social reconstruction.

In contrast to the romantic stands the realist, the dispassionate analyst of society as it is, willing to overlook moral flaws and social imperfections in favor of assembling and using political power for specifically designed purpose. Preoccupied with getting things done, the realist has little use for a politics of passionate moral indignation. A somewhat surprising example is furnished by the New Deal, surprising because it set out to overcome an economic crisis so deep that it seemingly should have produced a politics of passion. Yet it went about its business in a decidedly clinical and matter-of-fact manner. "Almost totally absent from the New Deal," writes Huntington, "were the moralism and Puritanism characteristic of creedal passion periods. The hallmark of the New Deal was pragmatism, opportunism, 'bold, persistent experimentation,' rather than the passionate reaffirmation of moral values. . . . The traditional moral virtues of politics did not rate high in the New Deal pantheon."[29]

When the term "realist" is used in politics these days, it invariably applies to the area of foreign policy. As if to confirm the instinctive American preference for goodness over greatness, the most famous of America's foreign policy realists were

associated with such Germanic names as Morgenthau, Kissinger, and Niebuhr (the last of whom, unlike the other two, was born in the United States). And even when it took American form—for example in the writings and doctrines of George F. Kennan—realism came accompanied by an aristocratic snobbishness toward democracy wildly at odds with the dominant trends in American political culture. Realism has always been something of an odd man out in the four traditions identified by Walter Russell Mead as shaping American foreign policy, too cynical for Wilsonianism, too interventionist for Jeffersonianism, and too elitist for Jacksonianism. Only with Hamilton and his offshoots have realists found an American tradition with which they can identify.

Given its minority status in the realm of ideas, realism has little in common with the themes of goodness that have run like a leitmotif through American political culture. On the surface, realism would seem to share the pessimistic view of human nature that follows naturally from American suspiciousness toward government, but only Morgenthau among the realist intellectuals was persuaded of the inherent ubiquity of human depravity; Niebuhr, by contrast, was, for all his emphasis on sin, a theorist of hope (as was Augustine, the theologian who most influenced his writing), and, as a liberal Protestant, he shared almost none of the premillennialism of the evangelicals who were his contemporaries.[30] The reason for this refusal to assume the worst about people is not too hard to find; realists, suspicious of the intentions of other states, recognized that for their own state to be able to be active in global affairs, confidence in, rather than suspicion of, government became essential. Realists are obviously not utopians, but neither

are they cynics. They would not be so insistent on the require-
ment that a society's foreign policy be guided by what is in
the national interest unless they were first persuaded that there
existed a nation whose interest was worth preserving.

Much the same is true when realists face the other features
of the American goodness agenda. Foreign policy realists are
moralism's greatest enemy; any state, they believe, faces potentially disastrous consequences if it allows its approach to the
world to be shaped by too sharp a distinction between good
and evil. At the same time, however, the realist cannot, in Ben-
thamite fashion, reduce all foreign policy decisions to calculations deduced from an abstract theory. Realists, like other advocates of national greatness, appeal to history and experience
rather than to systems and principles. It is precisely this distaste
for both moralism and theory that renders realism vulnerable
in domestic political debate; moralism leads to the charge of
hypocrisy when realists advocate tactics that run against American ideals (even as it distracts from the charge of hypocrisy
coming from the rest of the world by reducing the gap between
rhetoric and reality). In a democracy like the American one,
realists can hope to be successful, but they can never hope to
be popular. Their best opportunities arise when they work in
administrations more concerned with enhancing American
power than winning the next election. When politics is dominated by an excessive preoccupation with the results of public
opinion polls, they find themselves writing articles in magazines rather than sitting in the halls of power.

The correlation between a realistic outlook on the world and
the pursuit of American greatness is by no means perfect. Of
all those who worked assiduously on behalf of expanding

American power at home and abroad, Theodore Roosevelt was the most inclined to romanticism, as his Kiplingesque military exploits and explosively moralistic temperament attest.[31] Yet even Roosevelt shared some of the realist's distrust of holier-than-thou rejections of the fine arts of political compromise. It must not be forgotten that Roosevelt was no friend of the muckrakers. "To assail the great and admitted evils of our political and industrial life with such crude and sweeping generalizations as to include decent men in the general condemnation means the searing of the public conscience," he wrote. "There results a general attitude either of cynical belief in and indifference to public corruption or else of a distrustful inability to discriminate between the good and the bad."[32] With the partial exception of Roosevelt—a large exception, indeed—there can be little doubt that realism is the disposition most often identified with greatness, and romanticism the one most often associated with goodness.

On March 28, 1834, the U.S. Senate, led by Henry Clay, censured President Andrew Jackson based on his refusal to make available to Congress a paper he had read to his cabinet. Three years later, the Senate, now under the control of the Democratic Party, voted to expunge its earlier censure of the president. Beneath the partisanship and rhetoric, Daniel Walker Howe writes, stood two very different understandings of how the affairs of the Republic ought to be guided. Howe explains these differences by citing a July 1861 sermon by Horace Bushnell. For Bushnell, the "abstract-theoretical element," as he called it, was inferior to what he described as the "historic" tradition.

Whigs like Bushnell rejected approaches to politics that down-played the importance of history, whether they were the social contract theorists of the seventeenth century, the begin-the-world-anew sympathizers such as Thomas Paine and Thomas Jefferson, or the proponents of the state-sovereignty principles, such as Calhoun and advocates of hard-money policies, such as Andrew Jackson. In pretending that Jackson's censure never had happened, Democrats failed to recognize, in Bushnell's words, that "what any people can be and ought to be depends, in a principal degree, on what they have been."[33]

Along with ideas about human nature and attitudes toward rules and systems, approaches to history also determine an individual's or a political party's relationship to the idea of American greatness. Leaders who aspire to greatness invariably pay homage to the "mystic chains of memory" evoked by Abraham Lincoln. No better example is offered than Teddy Roosevelt, an amateur historian himself, who, as one of his many biographers writes, "worked with government agencies and the American Historical Association to preserve documents and to make sure professional history received its due as a major contributor to the interpretation of American life."[34] In a like-minded manner, the New Deal expressed its commitment to the idea of American greatness not only through its social programs and (eventually) its foreign policy, but also through projects such as the oral histories of the Federal Writers' Projects and the regional and local histories they sponsored. Even as late as the 1960s, John F. Kennedy, who aspired to greatness even if he never really achieved it, wrote (with or without help; it doesn't matter) a best-selling history of politicians singled out for their courage.

Presidents who seek to realize ideas of American greatness not only value history as an intellectual enterprise, they carry themselves like historical figures; they try to understand where they are in the chain of American leadership and how they can build on what their predecessors accomplished to advance their vision of what their country ought to be. Perhaps inspired by Mount Rushmore—imagine trying to find agreement in today's superheated partisan environment on whom should properly belong on such a monument—it is as if they know, even if they never quite say, that there will someday be built in Washington a testimony to them, and they want to ensure that the eventual monument will never lack a plentiful stream of visitors.

"History is bunk," Henry Ford once famously said, illustrating in a few well-chosen words the approach toward the past favored by those, such as Ford, for whom the ideal America was a village like that of Dearborn, Michigan (which, in characteristically American fashion, Ford did so much to destroy). There are obvious reasons why those who prefer a pure and virtuous America to a complex and complicated one turn their eyes away from the actual history of their country; respect for the facts of a society's existence is usually difficult to reconcile with romantic myths of innocent origins. One can, as a consequence, find numerous Americans, many of them populating the novels of Mark Twain and Henry James, who, in contrast to more decadent Europeans, do not want to be burdened by oppressive traditions. And much the same attitude toward America's past can be found among politicians and political parties who, in contrast to Lincoln, the Roosevelts, and Kennedy, show little interest in, and respect for, the history of their country. Although not enough history has gone by to make a definitive judgment, one of our leaders who most characteristically seems to share this obliviousness to history is our most recent.

Throughout his presidency, George W. Bush's approach to history has been eerily similar to those of the nineteenth-century Democrats who insisted on expunging the censure of Andrew Jackson from the historical record. Bush, of course, is a political conservative and, as such, has little in common with the inflammatory rhetoric of Paine, Jefferson, and Jackson. But he very much shares their radicalism when it comes to the question of how much the present is indebted to the past. As the revelations of former terrorism czar Richard Clarke made clear in early 2004, and as the September 11 commission eventually confirmed, the incoming Bush administration went out of its way not to listen to the accumulated experience of its predecessors, thereby paying relatively little attention to the gathering terrorist threat. Much the same approach to history characterized its military debacle in Iraq; convinced that American power could achieve any objective it chose, the planners of the Iraqi war not only failed to learn from the British experience in that country, they dismissed warnings from the U. S. State Department about such historically shaped realities as ethnic conflict and hostility to foreign occupation.

The hostility of the Bush administration toward history does not stop with foreign policy. Throughout his presidency, Mr. Bush has made secrecy in government a higher priority than access to historical records, incurring, with little or no unease, the enmity of professional historians. Unlike earlier presidents—Kennedy and Nixon, for example—he shows no inclination to take a stab at writing history, even with the assistance of his staff. In an interview with the television journalist Britt

Hume, Mr. Bush acknowledged that he never read newspapers, preferring instead to rely on the summaries provided by his office, and it is thus highly unlikely that he will pick up biographies or even the work of popular historians such as Stephen Ambrose. His approach to the environment ranks preservation well behind exploitation. His domestic policy breaks with more than half a century's commitment to using government to ensure a modicum of economic security to enter the uncharted, at least in recent times, waters of encouraging private-sector competition. Huge deficits produced by a combination of tax cuts and expensive subsidies to industry, which threaten to saddle subsequent generations with incalculable amounts of debt, treat the future with as little regard as the Bush administration treats the past. Of course history judgments are unpredictable, and Mr. Bush may come to be regarded as a figure who understood where America had come from and where it needed to go. But it is far more probable that Mr. Bush's insufficient respect for history will be viewed, if I am permitted to make a guess about the future, as one of the reasons why no great monument will ever be constructed to honor him.

◯— Should we then conclude from the Bush administration's disdain for history that, despite the assertions of William Kristol, David Brooks, and others, Mr. Bush does not properly belong in the camp of those who sought greatness for America? It is not difficult to understand why neoconservatives made the comparison in the first place. Unlike Bill Clinton, who never seemed comfortable exercising political power, the Bush administration has been determined not to show any signs of weakness in foreign policy, and, for all the discord and division that followed from the Iraq War, the one in Afghanistan seemed to many Americans a necessary, as well as impressive, response to the September 11 attack. The administration, moreover, clearly has not been hampered by traditional American concerns for weak and ineffective government in pursuit of its political objectives; adherence to the idea of the separation of powers or concerns to protect individual rights against the power of the state, distinctive features of eighteenth-century republicanism, are not prominent aspects of this administration's understanding of how power should be utilized. In his speeches and to some degree in his foreign policy actions, moreover, George W. Bush sounds like a cross between Theodore Roosevelt and Woodrow Wilson, not only committing troops to fight in wars abroad, but justifying their presence by invoking the power of democratic ideas. Mr. Bush, finally, is widely perceived among the American people as a forceful leader who responded effectively to terrorism, and no one could doubt his willingness, and that of his advisors, to take any steps necessary to ensure his reelection. From at least the end of the Truman presidency, Americans typically trust Republicans more than Democrats with national security, and to the extent that national security is a precondition for greatness, George W. Bush has some reason to be placed in that camp.

But only some reason. Measured across the whole span of what it takes to make a society great, President Bush more properly fits alongside that line of politicians who stood *against* invoking the ideals, and therefore paying for the costs, that would bring greatness to America. It is not so much over policy that the Bush administration finds its links with Jacksonian Democrats and anti–New Deal Republicans, although, despite his more interventionist foreign policy, those continuities do exist. The real reason the Bush administration does not fit in the great America camp involves its underlying philosophical assumptions about human nature and purpose.

Consider just a few of the similarities between the priorities of the Bush administration and those of earlier politicians and thinkers in the American goodness camp. While not much given to speculating about human nature, Mr. Bush's economic agenda is indebted to strongly asserted free market ideas that go far beyond Adam Smith in appreciating the ingenious ways in which individuals will always act out of selfish motives. He appointed as the head of the Department of Justice John Ashcroft, a Pentecostal whose views on the ubiquity of sin resonate with the premillennial theology of nineteenth-century evangelicals. For both economic and theological reasons, this is not an administration that appeals to the angels of anyone's better nature. True, there has been much talk about faith-based initiatives and the wonders they might be able to accomplish, but Mr. Bush as president rarely uses the language of compassionate conservatism so helpful to him in his campaigns for the presidency; he is as well known for not following through on his talk of compassion as he is for introducing the talk in the first place. The hope-filled language of the Reagan and Kennedy administrations finds no place among men like Vice President Dick Cheney, who are convinced that forces of darkness rule the world and must be met head-on with iron resolve. Suspicion and fear guide this administration, not confidence and generosity.

Hobbesian the Bush administration's view of the world may be, but realistic, in classic foreign policy terms, it is not. By invoking the term "axis of evil" in response to the terrorist attack on the United States, Mr. Bush signaled that his administration was prepared to turn its back on realpolitik, as least as public justification for its foreign policy, and put in its place the moralism of a Woodrow Wilson or Jimmy Carter. But this was a moralism for America only, not, as in previous administrations, a call for a better world in which others would share. Announcing from the very start of his presidency that he would not be bound by treaties on issues such as global warming and international courts, Mr. Bush has made clear that his foreign policy would be based on the honor-first unilateralist instincts of an Andrew Jackson, not the business-comes-first internationalism of Alexander Hamilton. For all the darkness of its vision, there is a romantic streak to Bush's view of the world; only a romantic committed to action for action's sake could persuade itself that toppling Saddam Hussein could be accomplished with little or no thought given to who and what would replace him. In the rhetoric of the administration's more enthusiastic spokesmen, such as Secretary of Defense Donald Rumsfeld, one hears echoes of the American West, as the go-it-alone, manly, and incorruptible hero confronts a foreign and decadent world with what to him is the simple sincerity of his plain-spoken truth.

Unlike a Calhoun, no commitment to systematic theory characterizes the Bush administration; even its adherence to laissez-faire did not prevent the president from rewarding favored industries with protection from free trade or stopping the free flow of domestic spending so long as political advantage flowed from it; indeed, for a true libertarian, this administration's commitments to expensive wars and even more expensive domestic reforms in energy and Medicare constitutes a nightmare. In addition, Mr. Bush, although quick to charge John F. Kerry with flip-flopping during the 2004 campaign, is more than willing to change positions for reasons of political expediency; he opposed creating a Department of Homeland Security only to shift ground and support it; he tried to hinder an investigation into the circumstances surrounding September 11 but backed down when his stance became politically awkward; and his announcements about the irrelevance of the United Nations would become muted—indeed, would disappear entirely—when he needed international support for his failed war in Iraq. For all these reasons, there is little in the Bush first term that resembles the tendency of goodness-oriented presidents from Andrew Jackson to Herbert Hoover to restrict their options out of observance to fixed principle.

Yet even without the theory, the Bush administration shares the inflexibility of those who have insisted upon the American goodness agenda. His is an administration of dogmatism without dogma, flexible to the point of wild inconsistency in its justifications for rigidly adhered-to policies like tax cuts while prepared to abandon tomorrow (without ever acknowledging that this is what it is doing) what only today was held to be matters of high principle. Rarely in American politics has an administration been as willing to do whatever has to be done to ensure reelection yet at the same time as insistent that it never listens to polls or changes its mind for reasons of political expediency.

No wonder, then, that missing from George W. Bush's campaign for reelection in 2004 were any significant promises of what he might do if elected for a second four years, replaced, in unprecedented fashion for an incumbent, by relentlessly negative attacks on his opponent.[35] Part of the explanation for this negativity, as Senator Kerry correctly charged, was financial; the Bush combination of tax cuts and increased spending rendered no new initiatives possible. But part of the explanation was also political, indeed prepolitical.

The attacks on John Kerry's patriotism launched by those close to the president, including Vice President Cheney, were anything but new in American history; scurrilous campaign rhetoric and accusations of disloyalty were prominent features of the political culture of the Jacksonian era as well as the McCarthy period. Whenever such attacks appear, they are suggestive of an outlook on the world that plays on American fears. Such forms of campaigning are invariably the work of those who put their careers and (especially these days) their ideologies ahead of their country, for when the campaign is over, the suspicion and distrust remain, rendering nearly impossible the kind of bipartisan cooperation that makes governance possible. Indeed, that may be the point: like radical tax-cutting, which leaves government unable to finance new programs, negative campaigning creates a situation in which politics never stops, deadlock never goes away, and policy—actual programs to help people lead better lives, feel more secure, and take pride in their society—never need be addressed. All this may sound overly cynical, but the political atmosphere in the first years of the twenty-first century is as hard-boiled and cynical as American politics can be.

It hardly seems appropriate to characterize this frenzy of nasty partisanship and bend-the-rules-to-your-own-benefit extremism an example of prioritizing goodness over greatness, for not much is good about it. But not only have fear-mongering and cynicism always been a feature of the goodness program in American political culture, George W. Bush utilizes such tactics in favor of a standpattist agenda that essentially holds that America has already achieved the good society and therefore has little or no need to experiment with anything new. If anything, American goodness, in the world according to Bush, was achieved much earlier in our history, in a period like the Gilded Age when businessmen were allowed to pursue what was best for them and in so doing presumably made America better for everyone. The task now is to return America to its goodness, not to advance it to its greatness, and for that, Mr. Bush's presidency seems particularly appropriate, for the only thing outsized and ambitious about Mr. Bush is his willingness to take whatever steps are necessary to repudiate the social reforms of the twentieth century that allowed so many Americans to feel a sense of membership in their national community. Having won two elections, Mr. Bush is entitled to be called a great politician. Having done so by paying so much attention to the means while exercising little or no responsible thought on the ends, he will never put into place a great America.

꙳— If American greatness were little more than a set of positions on the political issues of the day, presidents could legislate it into being so long as they chose the right policies designed to enhance it. But because greatness is a prepolitical quality, and because its assumptions about human nature, history, and reality have consistently taken second place to a preference for goodness in our political culture, the course of greatness in American history has always been uncertain and contingent. We now may be persuaded that the new society called the

United States had to create an effective national government; that the preservation of the Union and the abolition of slavery were essential to its continued existence; that some sense of order, including a role for government in the economy, was required to replace laissez-faire; that our habitual fear of entangling alliances would have to be put aside once it became clear that conflicts outside American borders inevitably involved American interests; that it was necessary to restore confidence during the Great Depression; and that passing the Civil Rights Act of 1964 could no longer be postponed. But each of those actions, however necessary, were controversial in their day—and some of them, such as the regulation of business and government, remain hotly contested down to the present. Prudence in nearly all these cases suggested not taking the course that eventually was taken. That those courses were taken at all suggests that the pursuit of greatness is typically impractical—and in some cases, such as the Democratic Party's commitment to civil rights, politically suicidal.

For reasons no one fully understands, each of America's great crises—the revolution and then the writing and ratification of the Constitution, the Civil War, and the Depression followed by World War II—took place at times when leaders committed to American greatness were in or were close to power. Not all of them, however, were considered candidates for greatness in advance; Lincoln was an obscure politician and minority president, and FDR was widely perceived as an intellectual lightweight. Given the opportunity, however, they rose to the occasion, and as tragic as were the events that launched them into greatness, both left the country more certain of its ideals and commitments and more poised to achieve them.

All of this suggests that September 11 easily could have been such a defining moment both for the United States—and for George W. Bush. Before the terrorist attack took place, American politics appeared to many as deadlocked, symbolized by the 2000 electoral debacle. And after the collapse of the Soviet Union, American foreign policy was also somewhat adrift, not only because of the lackluster commitments of the Clinton administration in Somalia and former Yugoslavia, but also because no defining post–Cold War program had emerged to shape foreign and defense priorities. Although clearly not well prepared intellectually for challenges of this magnitude, President Bush was given a chance both by Americans and by foreign leaders to fashion a vision of American greatness. At home, his family ties to an older Republican Party tradition of public service and noblesse oblige—the very tradition that had produced Theodore Roosevelt—might have allowed Mr. Bush to emphasize the necessity for all Americans to share equally in the response to the terrorist attack; no politician, certainly not Ronald Reagan, Bill Clinton, or even Mr. Bush's father, was in a better position to declare the culture war over than the president who was in power when an act of real war took place on American shores. And in much the same manner, the fact that the attack was launched, not by a state, but by terrorists who operate from murky corners of the globe, demanded a reaction that required international cooperation brought about by equal vulnerability to attack above and beyond any military campaigns designed to invade and replace already existing states.

None of this, of course, actually happened, as Mr. Bush instead has opted to pursue policies that divided Americans from one another and divided America from the rest of the world, as if the country, and indeed the entire globe, could be governed from one little corner of the American ideological spectrum. In this, there stands a lesson to be learned about American greatness. Everything else being equal, greatness is so hard to realize that it will never find its way naturally to the top of the priorities established by American political culture; it takes leadership ability to put it there. George W. Bush's presidency demonstrates that rejecting greatness when it is providentially offered takes as much leadership, if of a particularly perverse sort, as finding it when the conditions barely exist. Mr. Bush has not been prevented from unifying the country around its ideals of liberty and equality by powerful private interests, a misinformed public, partisan deadlock, or overseas obstruction; on the contrary, given a clear path to leadership, he instead has decided to put obstacles in the path of greatness by strengthening private interests, engaging in systematic misinformation about his means and ends, working so hand-in-glove with one party as to deny the other its place at the bargaining table, and transforming a sympathetic world into a hostile one. In so doing, George W. Bush has not only lost his own opportunity to make America great, he has made more difficult, through future deficits and endless partisan retribution, the ability of any of his immediate successors to do so as well. It is an accomplishment, to be sure, but one unlikely to be recalled by future historians as fashioning an America of which a Marshall, a Lincoln, or either of the Roosevelts would have been proud.

III Conservatism's Retreat
from Greatness

Only one approach to constitutional law, writes Robert Bork, whose failure to win confirmation as a justice to the U.S. Supreme Court in 1987 helped ignite the contemporary culture war, "is consonant with the design of the American Republic." Bork's preferred method, original intent, holds "that a judge is to apply the Constitution according to the principles intended by those who ratified the document."[1] Anything else, especially any theory that allows judges to apply their own ideologies and preferences to the decisions they are called upon to reach, ends in tyranny.

Original intent applies not only to the Constitution, but, in the eyes of some contemporary conservatives, to ordinary legislation. That, at least, is the conclusion reached by Justice Antonin Scalia in his discussion of *Church of Holy Trinity v. United States* (1892). At issue was the effort by a New York City church to appoint as its rector an Englishman, thereby running afoul of a statute making it illegal to "assist or encourage the importation or migration of any alien" into the United States by holding out the promise of a job. The Court held that the law was never meant to exclude such a deserving person and ought not to be enforced. Scalia offered a contrary view. Even a bad law is still a law, he said, and we are obligated to follow what it says whether we like it or not: "the text is the law, and it is the text that must be observed."[2] Scalia's views on the matter came under attack by the anthropologist Vincent Crapanzano, who cited his discussion as a good example of a naive and logically contradictory approach to interpretation.[3] Original intent, Crapanzano pointed out, does not offer a fixed standard that can serve as an inoculation against interpretation but is itself an interpretation, one with its own, often divisive and partisan, view of the decisions judges ought to be taking.

It would be difficult to find an idea associated with contemporary conservatism that has had more staying power than original intent. During the 2000 political campaign that eventually made him president, George W. Bush praised Antonin Scalia and Clarence Thomas and promised to do all in his power to appoint more judges like them. He continued to emphasize the same point after assuming office. "I'm going to put strict constructionists on the bench," he said during the 2002 Congressional elections. "We need people . . . in the United States Senate who will work with the White House to have a solid judiciary, to make sure that the judges do what they're supposed to do in the United States and not overstep their bounds."[4] During his 2004 reelection campaign, the president, who saw political advantage in such "wedge" issues as gay marriage and stem cells, made attacks on judicial tyranny part of his performance in the presidential debates. On this point, Mr. Bush has been consistent. The men and women he nominated were in near unanimous agreement that the duty of a judge is to apply the law, not to make it.

What interests me about this fidelity to original intent is not whether it offers an interpretation-free standard by which laws can be judged; I agree with Crapanzano that it does not. I instead take the doctrine to signify the extraordinary lengths to which contemporary conservatives will go to distance themselves from ideas about American greatness. For there can be doubt that the true enemies of strict construction are not the Warren Court liberals of the early twenty-first century but the nationalistic Federalists of the early nineteenth. No one would have looked at the ideas of Robert Bork and Antonin Scalia with more astonishment at their pernicious quality than John Marshall.

Marshall is as conservative a thinker as one can find in the American pantheon. Besides Abraham Lincoln, he is also the leader most responsible for the fact that contemporary Americans live in a society whose government is capable of formulating and achieving ambitious national objectives. And he was an uninhibited judicial activist whose opinions owed more to his ability to read his political objectives into texts than they owed fidelity to those texts. How could someone whose politics are so agreeable to contemporary conservatives as John Marshall have developed an approach to Constitutional interpretation so distasteful? "An explanation of some sort is required," Bork writes, the words "of some sort" suggesting that he is about to offer a lame one. Lame it certainly is. Bork claims that while Marshall stretched the meaning of laws—something for which Scalia, although not Bork, would presumably condemn him—he was nonetheless faithful to the Constitution. But there was nothing in the Constitution about the Supreme Court assuming the authority of judicial review, as Marshall did in *Marbury v. Madison.* Nor could the expansive view of commerce adopted by Marshall in *Gibbons v. Ogden* be found in our founding document. As if to recognize the need to shift his defense of Marshall in the face of these realities, Bork concludes that while Marshall may indeed have been a judicial activist, he was writing at a time when the "entire enterprise" called America that was in danger.[5] Under such dramatic circumstances, Bork suggests, some form of judicial activism may be necessary to save the country.

The problem with this line of reasoning is that no one has been more insistent on the current dangers facing the United States than Robert Bork. Indeed, it is not only America but all of Western civilization that "are in peril in ways not previously seen," he writes at the start of *Slouching Toward Gomorrah.*[6] If we apply a Borkian reading to Bork—"not previously seen" unambiguously means never before happened—his words suggest that the "slide into a modern, high-tech version of the Dark Ages," as he calls it, will be worse than Nazism and Soviet Communism, all of which makes the squabbles between the Federalists and Jeffersonians of Marshall's day seem rather insignificant. It is characteristic of those who believe in the essentiality of American goodness to conclude that contemporary America is the embodiment of badness; whatever the other differences between conservatives, all of them believe that America can only be made good again if it is forced to take dramatic steps to reverse its decline into decadence. It is fair to say that no other thinker in American life has been as forceful in his denunciations of what the United States has become than Robert Bork.

A conservative might conclude that a crisis this serious requires at the very least some form of judicial activism as a remedy; perhaps Justices Scalia and Thomas believed something along these lines when they invoked the equal protection clause, thereby assuming the mantle of judicial activism, to seal Mr. Bush's ascension to the presidency in 2000. Bork, to his credit, is more principled than they are; while generally supporting the decision, he did worry that *Bush v. Gore* might "federalize state election laws."[7] As admirable as his intellectual consistency may be, however, his refusal to bend on his strict constructionist views, when combined with his conviction that the United States has so desperately lost its sense of goodness, leads him to a position far more dangerous than the Constitution-stretching proclivities of John Marshall.

Original intent is defended by Bork as necessary for democracy; without it, he claims, unelected judges will be free to impose their will on the country as a whole. But original intent also can be quite undemocratic if it is used, as Bork would use it, to disallow a people's capacity to choose the amount of economic regulation they want, the extent to which ideas about equality should be applied in practice, or the proper distribution of powers between the states and the federal government. No wonder, then, that Bork adopts a methodology so at odds with Marshall's, for original intent is meant as a restraint on the national greatness Marshall sought; following its principles would preclude any creative political leadership that attempted to respond to contingencies unforeseen by the founders. Bork writes as if inside every leader there is a Lincoln or a Roosevelt struggling to get out, and the best way to prevent that from happening is by insisting on a set of rules of Constitutional interpretation that would keep them in. We need original intent because we are Faustian creatures who, if permitted, will create new worlds we think wonderful but that, without our realizing it, will condemn us to darkness.

As much as Bork hopes that we might avoid such a fate by committing ourselves to original intent, he knows that, modern creatures as we are, we are unlikely ever to do so; even the election of conservative Republicans like the first George Bush and Ronald Reagan were unable to stop the tide. What should a conservative do when departures from original intent become so common? Unlike Marshall, who used an expansive form of interpretation to push the Court toward conservative positions, Bork would use a conservative form of interpretation to advance the Court, and the United States, in a radical direction. Railing against the ambition of those with whom he is in such vehement disagreement,

Bork reveals ambitions of his own. His, though, are negative ones; he goes beyond efforts to impose restraints on American greatness to suggestions that, at least in its present form, America does not deserve any greatness that might inadvertently come its way.

Bork has written that when the Court reached one of its recent decisions—the Virginia Military Institute case that banned sex discrimination at a state-funded military academy—his wife told him that the judges were a "band of outlaws." He found himself agreeing with her. "An outlaw is a person who coerces others without warrant in law," he wrote. "That is precisely what a majority of the present Supreme Court does." When such illegal actions are taken, we require, at the very least, a constitutional amendment, or even a series of them, that will overturn all of Marshall's major rulings, as well as just about all of the jurisprudence fashioned by the Supreme Court in the years since Marshall's death. "Decisions of courts," as Bork puts is, "might be made subject to modification or reversal by majority vote of the Senate and the House of Representatives. Alternatively, courts might be deprived of the power of constitutional review." Yet even these steps, radical as they are in a society that has rarely chosen to amend its constitution, might not be enough. "Perhaps," Bork continues, "an elected official will one day simply refuse to comply with a Supreme Court decision." This sounds precariously close to a call for civil disobedience, which Bork acknowledges may sound "shocking." (It does, I confess, to me, but, then again, I am nearly always shocked that a man of Bork's intemperate disposition and volatile language was ever considered for the U.S. Supreme Court.) But since the activists on the court have already engaged in civil disobedience themselves, dramatic action is required to counter them.[8]

Bork's views appeared in a symposium published by the magazine *First Things*, which prefaced his comments by asking "whether we have reached or are reaching the point where conscientious citizens can no longer give moral assent to the existing regime."[9] Such inflammatory rhetoric was too much for conservatives like Gertrude Himmelfarb and Walter Berns, who saw in the editor's remarks the revolutionary nihilism of 1960s leftism reborn on the right and resigned from the editorial board of the magazine.[10] As far as conservative attitudes toward American greatness go, the publication of this symposium constituted an important watershed. On one side stood those who shared the idea that things have gone terribly wrong with America, but who could never bring themselves, as William Bennett put it in his critique of regime talk, to confuse America with Amerika. And just as clearly on the other side stood conservatives whose disgust with America's loss of goodness led them to question whether America's continued existence as a democracy had reached an end.

Bork belongs to the latter group. True, he distanced himself from the *First Things* comment that the "American regime" was "illegitimate." Yet he not only pronounced duly appointed and confirmed U.S. Supreme Court judges outlaws, he twice used the term "illegitimate" to describe their approach to the Constitution and he wrote darkly of a "supine" America that was "willing to watch democracy slip away." It is not difficult to understand why Bork is so pessimistic for his country. As his defense of original intent suggests, Bork is appalled at the expansive procedures used by judges to reach their decisions. But, as his comments about the decadence of American culture indicate, he is distraught as well about the substance of the decisions they reach; a court that extends rights to a woman to control her own body or grants the right to marry to homosexuals or believes that universities may be allowed to take race into account in their admissions decisions is reaching the wrong conclusions whatever the methodology it employs. The two ideals that have long stood as the goals toward which a great America might strive—liberty and equality—are

precisely the goals that America, in Bork's view, must do everything to avoid.

If he were just a defender of original intent, Bork would be the
heir of a long tradition of American conservatism that includes
the anti-Federalists, Calhoun, and the judges who opposed Roosevelt's New Deal. But by arguing so forcefully against liberty and
equality, Bork distances himself from his own society in ways
strikingly similar to those of the 1960s radicals he so frequently
denounces. Indeed the parallels with the period he detests are
striking. Bork writes that the "best strategy" for those who share
his understanding of how rotten America has become is "to attempt to create small islands of decency and civility in the midst
of a subpagan culture."[11] (Home schooling and gated communities—let's call them communes of the right—are his examples of
the kinds of places to which the few good people remaining in
America ought to retreat.) If conservatives today sound like
Charles Reich and Theodore Rozsak, advocates of a similar withdrawal from mainstream life that marked the counterculture of
the New Left, that only indicates that the conviction that we have
lost our way crosses the usual ideological boundaries. In whatever
form it takes, however, the idea that America has wandered so far
from the path of the good and true that it has little hope for
redemption is incompatible with the idea that America is, or will
soon become, a society on the path to greatness.

⌒— One might be tempted to conclude that Bork's position
is about as far as a conservative can go in denying the possibility
of American greatness. One would be wrong. Bork, let us re-
member, strongly defends the original intent of the ratifiers of
the Constitution. But some American conservatives think that

the Constitution itself contained serious mistakes. These were not mistakes of understatement that made it necessary for a John Marshall to come along and specify powers the national government ought rightly to have had but did not. They were instead mistakes of overemphasis that gave the national government far too much power to begin with. I will call this persistent strain of conservative unhappiness with the Constitution "Calhounism," after its most famous expositor.

Given the symbolic importance the Constitution had assumed in American life, John C. Calhoun did try his best to show that there is no inherent conflict between his views and those embedded in that document. In no sense did the Constitution create a national government, he insisted; the government it formed, like the one under the Articles of Confederation it replaced, was federalist. The United States, Calhoun told his readers, is not a nation in the usual sense; it is instead "the government of a community of States, and not the government of a single State or nation." "Community" was the operative word here. Although difficult to imagine today, when slavery is considered America's great evil, for Calhoun the Southern way of life, and in particular its rejection of Lockean liberalism in favor of an emphasis on organic wholeness, was the only good and virtuous alternative to the nationalism toward which America was rushing. The option was open to the founders to divest the states of their sovereignty and, in so doing, to merge the states "into one great community or nation," Calhoun wrote, but this the framers wisely chose not to do.[12]

Despite this attempt to be faithful to the Constitution, however, Calhoun concluded that the framers were sometimes wrong as they confronted the problems they were trying to address. He emphasized two mistakes in particular. The first is that they presumed that the most intense conflicts in the society would be between large states and small ones, but in fact the single biggest conflict turned out to be a sectional one in which both large and small states could be found on each side of the divide. An ever more serious mistake lay "in constituting a single instead of a plural executive." The framers would have been wiser to have structured the executive office into two parts and required the concurrence of both before a bill could become a law, a typically Calhounian move to insulate the South from Northern political superiority. In defense of the plural executive, Calhoun was willing to rewrite nearly all the agreements hammered out in Philadelphia. Let one be in charge of foreign affairs and the other in charge of domestic concerns, he muses at one especially speculative point, and let "the selection . . . be decided by lot." The purpose of having an executive, in Calhoun's view, was to ensure balance between different interests, but this "has entirely failed, and, by its failure, done much to disturb the whole system and to bring about the present dangerous state of things."[13]

What is to be done when the Constitution is wrong? Calhoun could have answered, along Borkian lines, that the proper response is amend it, as many times as necessary. Instead, he offered a sweeping view of Constitutional interpretation that outdid anything found in John Marshall.

It is for us who see and feel it to do what the framers of the Constitution would have done had they possessed the knowledge in this respect which experience has given to us, that is, provide against the dangers which the system has practically developed; and which, had they been foreseen at the time and left without guard, would undoubtedly have prevented the States, forming the southern section of the Confederacy, from ever agreeing to the Constitution; and which, under like circumstances, were they now out of, would prevent them from entering into the Union.[14]

Calhoun's meaning could not be clearer. The Southern states agreed to the Constitution because they thought they were being offered iron-clad guarantees that they would be permitted to retain slavery in perpetuity. As far as any could see at the time, they were right to do so; the Constitution gave them everything they wanted in this regard, which is why they signed on. But human beings not being gods, certain events were unanticipated, including the geographic expansion of the United States and the increasing unhappiness in the North with slavery. Now that we know these things to have happened, Calhoun argued, we have every right to go back to a document that (in his view) was already federal rather than national and transform it even further away from any conception of a national polity into one even more federal.

Calhoun's treatment is about as far from Borkian original intent as one can go; in matters of Constitutional faith, to use Sanford Levinson's rich metaphor, Bork looks like a fundamentalist while Calhoun resembles an atheist.[15] Yet both are fearful of the exercise of national authority and are willing to use whatever means are at hand to prevent its exercise. Before the Civil War, the best way to restrain the exercise of national power was to rewrite the Constitution to make it more like the Polish Parliament. After the Civil War, such restraints were best guaranteed by insisting that the eighteenth century binds the twenty-first. However different Calhoun and Bork may be in approach, they are quite similar in their end results.

In spite of his lack of reverence toward documents so often invoked by conservatives—besides the Constitution, Calhoun was perfectly willing to throw out much of the analysis contained in the *Federalist Papers*—Calhounism continues to exercise a powerful fascination over the conservative mind. Willmoore Kendall, a conservative political theorist immortalized in fiction by Saul Bellow as Mr. Mosby long before Allan Bloom would be featured in *Ravelstein*, proposed ideas remarkably similar to those of Calhoun. Or so charges Harry Jaffa, one of the twentieth century's leading Straussian political philosophers.[16] Jaffa's ire was provoked by a comment made by Kendall in his 1964 lectures at Vanderbilt University which were posthumously transformed into a book by him and George Carey. In that book, Kendall and Carey claimed that the American political tradition had been "derailed" by Abraham Lincoln when, at Gettysburg, Lincoln dated the creation of the United States to 1776 rather than 1787 and in so doing elevated equality to a place it never had in the American founding. "To fix upon the Declaration and to extract from it our basic commitment in the manner that Lincoln has done," Kendall and Carey wrote, "cannot help but create a distorted picture of our tradition."[17] If we substitute Jefferson for Lincoln, Jaffa charged, we find ourselves in Calhoun territory, for Calhoun also made the case that the equality language of the Declaration was not binding on later generations.

Lincoln, it is widely recognized, was not a believer in racial equality the way that term is understood today; his views of African Americans, especially those expressed in his debates with Stephen A. Douglas, are patronizing and offensive to contemporary ears. Nor would Lincoln necessarily have endorsed anything like the Populist demands for equality in the late nineteenth century; Lincoln himself died before economic and social equality became burning issues, but his private secretary John Hay did live long enough to confront those issues and wound up in the decidedly inegalitarian position of avidly supporting big corporations.

Nonetheless, Lincoln believed that the preservation of the United States required at the very least a symbolic commitment to the ideal of equality, and his most famous speech—indeed, America's most famous speech—offered just that.

For Willmoore Kendall, following in this regard Eric Voegelin, symbols are anything but trivial; they are "the *first* order of business for the political scientist."[18] Make a symbolic commitment to equality, Kendall believed, and before long you will have "a series of Abraham Lincolns, each prepared to insist that those who oppose this or that new application of the equality standard are denying the possibility of self-government."[19] (Kendall's list of would-be Lincolns includes Washington and Jefferson before him and the two Roosevelts and John F. Kennedy after him.)[20] Since the inevitable result of such a development will be completely absurd notions of equality—for Kendall an example might be the "one person, one vote" doctrine announced by the Supreme Court in *Reynolds v. Sims* (1964)—Lincoln was playing with fire when he let the equality demon out of the bag at Gettysburg. Most conservatives find equality in practice problematic; Kendall, unlike Jaffa, finds it problematic in theory as well. He was not Calhounian if by that term is meant a defense of slavery. But he surely was Calhounian if the term means the conviction that even sacred American texts expressing the idea of equality are mistaken and ought to be ignored.

Whatever Kendall's degree of Calhounism, other writers in the American political tradition rose to the defense of the American South and its distinctive way of life in ways that strongly resembled the South Carolinian. For them, the South was the only region of the United States capable of resisting trends in the direction of progress, bigness, and overseas expansion. "The American industrial system is expanding faster than the nation and the world can absorb it," wrote Herman Clarence Nixon, one of the twelve contributors to *I'll Take My Stand*, first published in 1930. "Speed in a dangerous direction or in a vicious circle is no virtue," he continued, "and the South can well afford to be backward in a movement toward an internal collapse or an external collision." For Nixon, a term like "provincial" was a compliment. Rejecting Henrik Ibsen's "master builder," Nixon offered no apology for the refusal of Southerners to engage in creating anything "to dizzy heights beyond their power to surmount and envisage."[21]

Richard Weaver was an undergraduate at Vanderbilt when the young professors in the English Department produced *I'll Take My Stand*, and his eventual contribution to the debate was even more vehement in its defense of the South and its attack on all things Northern. John P. East, a political scientist who served as the junior senator from North Carolina during the 1980s—the senior one at the time was Jesse Helms—described Weaver as "the founding father" of modern American conservatism, a sentiment shared by many other twentieth-century conservative intellectuals, including Frank Meyer and Willmoore Kendall.[22] *Ideas Have Consequences*, published in 1948, is indeed a seminal volume, for in it Weaver deals honestly with a dilemma that has plagued American conservative thought since World War II. That dilemma can be expressed syllogistically: Conservatives, none more so than Weaver, detest modernity. America is the very embodiment of modernity. Must conservatives therefore, for all their professed patriotism, also detest America?

Perhaps Weaver did not detest the United States, but he certainly disliked what it had become. The year in which his major book was published, 1948, was also the year in which the Cold War between the Soviet Union and the United States reached its crescendo. Contemplating the emerging Cold War, Weaver, it seems clear in retrospect, was a defeatist. Western liberalism was characterized by a "fundamental incapacity to think, arising from an inability to see contradictions," and this in turn "deprives it of the power to propagate," he wrote. The Soviets had no such problems. "Soviet Communism . . . despite its ostensible commitment to materialism, has generated a body of ideas with a terrifying power to spread." In his efforts to define the American advantages in the Cold War, Richard Nixon bragged of the kitchen appliances we had that they did not. But Weaver blamed our weakness on what Nixon understood, rightly it turns out, to be our strength. Preoccupied with material things, Americans, Weaver believed, were like spoiled children, resentful of anyone who would presume to discipline them for their own good. (Even the military draft, in Weaver's view, "looks suspiciously like bribing the child with candy," because it offered people benefits in return for military service.) In contrast to us, the Soviets had no tolerance for spoiled brats. "The Russians with habitual clarity of purpose have made their choice; there is to be discipline, and it is to be enforced by the elite controlling the state."[23] A strong defender of private property, Weaver was certainly not endorsing communism. But nor could he bring himself to believe that American society, which had long ago left behind the chivalric codes of his honor-bound South in favor of what he called Megalopolis, possessed any form of greatness worth passionate defense in its confrontation with Soviet power.

Every now and then a thinker with views similar to those of Kendall or Weaver will enter the public's consciousness. Perhaps the most famous example occurred in 1981 when President Ronald Reagan considered naming M. E. Bradford to the chairmanship of the National Endowment for the Humanities. Nominations such as these often shed light on the obscure writings of a previously unknown person. (Later, under Bill Clinton, Lani Guinier's law review articles would receive similar treatment.) In Bradford's case, public curiosity quickly revealed a man who compared Lincoln to Oriental despots, accused him of being "touched by a Bonapartist sense of destiny," denounced the "millenarian infection" he had spread, and charged that Lincoln's Second Inaugural was not an appeal to bind the wounds of the war but a form of "rhetorical manicheanism" designed to continue the South's oppression. Charges of racial insensitivity followed, ones that, at least in my view, were quite legitimate. But there existed an additional reason to question Bradford's appointment to an organization with the word "national" in its title; in opposing Lincoln so vigorously, Bradford also opposed the nation Lincoln helped bring into existence. Combine the idea of equality with the idea of union, Bradford argued, and you get, not a nation-state capable of aspiring to great things, but "a juggernaut powerful enough to arm and enthrone any self-made Caesar we might imagine: even an unprepossessing country lawyer from Illinois."[24] As conservative as William Bennett is, Bradford was too conservative for him; Bennett, and many other neoconservatives opposed Bradford's appointment, and it was never made.

If Bradford is any indication, Calhoun's legacy is antinationalistic, yet Calhoun began his political career as an American nationalist. In *The Southern Tradition*, Eugene Genovese reminds us that Calhoun's intellectual roots are not properly Jeffersonian; the great nullifier once shared the conservative worldview of Federalists like Joseph Story and, to a surprising extent, John Marshall. Even though both Story and Calhoun were antidemocratic, equally opposed to Andrew Jackson, and similar in their religious convictions, they would at the time of the Missouri Compromise part ways, and what divided them was the Federalist contention that, in Genovese's words, "an aspirant great power required a high level of political centralization."[25]

Genovese tries his best to defend the vision of American goodness associated with Calhoun and his intellectual descendents such as Weaver, but he is unconvincing. Calhoun, facing a choice between slavery and American greatness, opted without hesitation for the former. Even Genovese's sympathetic portrait of M. E. Bradford leaves no doubt that, faced with a choice similar to Calhoun's, he made a similar decision; "since they support the rights of the community against the claims of the centralized state," Genovese writes of Southern conservatives like Bradford, "they have had to bow to the wishes of racist communities."[26] But no one has to bow to racism if he chooses not to; Bradford could have ranked his priorities differently and concluded that if the community admired by him and his fellow Southerners was stained with the sin of racism, his job would be to educate in the hope of redeeming them; an opponent of all equality in general including racial equality, however, this was not something he was prepared to do. The alternative America defended by Calhoun and his subsequent followers is not only hopelessly romantic and constitutionally impossible, it is based on the superiority of one race over another, differing only over whether such inequalities take the form of slavery or legally permissible segregation. Is it any wonder that the Southern tradition, so long as America envisioned itself a great society committed to equality for all, stood for so long in the corner of obscurity from which Genovese is trying to rescue it?

The American South, while containing far more than its fair share of reactionaries, also yields up thinkers such as the Genoveses or John Shelton Reed, whose vision of community does not tolerate racial injustice. Yet no matter how impressive their scholarship, they too face a dilemma like the one that confronted the more unyielding defenders of the South. For even if we evoke the organic holism or, in Genovese's case, the anticapitalism, of the Old South, while putting in brackets its treatment of African Americans, defending it still means dismissing America's increasing cosmopolitanism, social heterogeneity, industrial prowess, technological dynamism, and global influence. Calhoun's legacy is to leave a way of thinking about America that emphasizes the presumed goodness of its past without appreciating the real accomplishments of its present and future.

◇— The South itself has not been willing to cooperate with those intent on idealizing it. Three of every ten Americans now live in the South, as its population in the 1990s increased considerably faster than the population increase for the United States as a whole. Once economically backward, the South is home to sprawling exurban communities housing some of America's fastest-growing industries and the people who work for them. Richard Weaver and M. E. Bradford would feel as uncomfortably alien in North Carolina's Research Triangle Park or Disney's Epcot Center as they would in Yankee Stadium.

The coming of modernity to the South resulted in changes political as well as demographic, bringing an end to Democratic Party domination and replacing it with an emerging Republican majority. It should be good news for the achievement of American greatness that the one region in the country most strongly fearful of national power has migrated to the party that throughout most of its early history stood for the principle of national unity. This, however, turns out not to be the case, for as Earl and Merle Black write in their history of the phenomenon, this "growing Republican Party . . . owed little to Abraham Lincoln but much to Goldwater and even more to Reagan."[27] On the question of national greatness, the parties switched sides between the mid–nineteenth and mid–twentieth centuries, as the Republicans, once identified with a strong nation, became the party of low taxes and small government while the Democrats, formerly the sectionalist party of Lincoln's rival Stephen A. Douglas, adopted the program of strong government and national unity that the Republicans had abandoned.[28] The South's political transformation is therefore more apparent than real. A hundred years ago, Southerners voted overwhelmingly for a party that stood against the idea of a strong America. Now they continue to do exactly that. The only difference is that the name of the party for which they tend to vote has changed.

Southerners retain a degree of Calhoun's early nationalism right into the twenty-first century; this is a region in which military culture is strong, as is a patriotic sense that citizens owe their loyalty to the decisions of the commander in chief. But there has always been a contingent character to Southern nationalism, especially among conservatives who, in the spirit of Calhoun, were nationalists only to the degree that the American nation accepted Southern distinctiveness as part of its identity. (Southern liberals, like Lyndon Johnson, typically wanted the South to share the benefits of modernity being showered on the rest of the country.) Now that Republicans are emerging as the dominant conservative party in the region, the South's claim to be the most patriotic region of the United States is as powerful as ever, but the contingent character of Southern nationalism has not changed; if anything, it has been strengthened.

As the Republican Party became more competitive in the South, race begun to play less of a role in the region's politics.

Of course racial appeals have not disappeared, especially because so many conservative Republicans were once segregationist Democrats; ties to explicit racists brought the downfall of
Senate Majority Leader Trent Lott of Mississippi. Still, Lott
was replaced by Bill Frist of Tennessee, a physician far more
interested in the intricacies of Medicare than in the power of
White Citizens' Councils. This transformation surely represents good news, for any decline in explicit racism is always to
be welcomed. But the increasing salience of economic issues
among Southern Republicans has consequences for American
greatness more serious in some ways than the decreasing vibrancy of racist views once associated with Southern Democracy. Unlike in the past, when Southern Democrats did not ask
that the entire country commit itself to segregation but were
content if the South was left alone to keep the races separate,
today's Republicans believe that the low-wage, nonunion, ex-
port-driven, unregulated but highly subsidized economy of
North Carolina or Texas ought to be a model for the country
as a whole. Their support for the nation is contingent on the
whole nation becoming more like the South.

Oddly enough, the entire country *is* becoming more like the
South. Once symbolic of a nostalgic past, the South's approach
to capitalism now seems the wave of the future; fast-growing
states in the Southwest and West are strongly committed to laissez-faire, and with the decline of manufacturing and unions in
the Midwest and North, the same ideas are making themselves
heard in quarters from which they were absent for more than
half a century. The South, which waited so patiently for the
North's Lincolnesque zeal for equality to pass, and when it did
quickly reestablished its practice of racial superiority, was

also willing, somewhat more impatiently, for the Rooseveltian mission of economic regulation also to pass, after which, if they have their way, the American economy will come to resemble a Southern preference for libertarianism that runs from Richard Weaver to Tom DeLay.

As economics goes, politics cannot be far behind. Since the North has historically been the home of those advocating a strong government capable of acting in the national interest, the arrival of a Southern-dominated Republican Party on the national scene has been accompanied by an effort to revisit, and where possible reverse, the steps by which a national state came into existence in the United States. "Southern conservatives had never accepted the terms of the mid–twentieth century social contract known as the New Deal," Michael Lind has written.[29] (Dick Armey, a former Republican House Majority Leader from Texas, as if to prove that Richard Weaver was not the only conservative to admire the self-confidence of dictatorships, wrote in 1995 that the New Deal and Great Society on the one hand and the Five-Year Plan and Great Leap Forward on the other were created by "the same sort of person," the only differences between them being those of "power and nerve.")[30] As Lind also notes, "George W. Bush was not the first Texan to be elected president, nor the first conservative to be elected president. But he was the first Texan conservative to be elected president."[31] Texan conservatives, one might say, are the genuine thing; in their 2002 party platform, for example, they hold that "the United States of America is a Christian nation" and they call for "the abolition of federal agencies involved in activities not originally intended to be delegated to the federal government under a strict interpretation of the

Constitution."[32] This is pretty radical stuff, but Texas Republicans are unashamed; understanding the opportunity George W. Bush's reelection presents to them, Republicans with ideas such as these are now engaged in a systematic attempt to reverse the New Deal, and with it the equality that enabled Americans from all social classes to feel a sense of membership in a common national enterprise. The term used by its advocates to describe this objective—federalism—has Calhounian roots. But unlike Calhoun's sectionalism, its consequences are being felt in every region of the country.

Organizations like the Federalist Society have emerged to become the intellectual center of the new conservative reevaluation of the role of the nation-state. As Federalist Society thinkers understand the issue, the growth of a strong national government was fueled by two important constitutional trends. One was the New Deal program that allowed the federal government to regulate industry on behalf of national objectives. The other was a century-long process of applying the Fourteenth Amendment to the states. Contemporary federalists want to reverse both of them.

Conservatives typically claim that their primary objective in reversing these two trends is to confront something they call liberalism, but in fact government regulation of the economy and the expansion of the equality guarantees of the Fourteenth Amendment were not products of liberalism but outgrowths of trends that have long had bipartisan support in the United States. New Deal economic policies had their intellectual roots in Hamilton's and Marshall's willingness to regulate commerce in the interests of economic growth and would be ratified by Republican presidents in the years after the Supreme Court endorsed them. The Fourteenth Amendment was the crowning glory of nineteenth-century Republicanism and was brought to the states with great energy by a Republican Supreme Court justice named Earl Warren. In attacking both developments, conservatives are using the language of federalism in the hope of returning America to a society that would have more in common with eighteenth-century anti-Federalists and the stuck-in-the-mud Democrats of the early nineteenth century than with nation-building Federalists like John Marshall and Daniel Webster.

The Supreme Court—more properly the five judges who constitute a majority on the Supreme Court—has taken the lead in applying this misnamed Federalist jurisprudence. In a series of cases starting with *United States v. Lopez* (1995), the Court, which for half a century had shied away from passing on the constitutionality of national legislation, began to scrutinize, and to find wanting, acts of Congress.[33] Lopez itself ruled that Congress had no authority to ban firearms within local school zones. *City of Boerne v. Flores* threw out the Religious Freedom Restoration Act, an effort by Congress to protect the free exercise of religion in the face of an earlier Court decision that appeared to limit it.[34] Warming to its task, the Court then invalidated key portions of the Brady Handgun Violence Protection Act and held that the application of the Americans with Disabilities Act to the states was unconstitutional.[35] And, in the case that received the most national attention, the Court ruled that Congress did not have the power to enforce the Fourteenth Amendment against the states even when a state failed to protect the rights of a particular individual, in this case a woman who was raped and believed that the Violence

Against Women Act had given her national protection against the state's failure to do so.[36] Lately, the Court has moderated its state sovereignty fervor, for example by declining to rule invalid the Family and Medical Leave Act in 2003,[37] which suggests that even once-strong advocates for this combination of federalism and libertarianism are having their doubts. But that just makes even more important the fact that George W. Bush's likely chance to appoint the next few judges to the U.S. Supreme Court will have a major say in how committed the United States will remain to the principle of national sovereignty.

As the court's second thoughts might suggest, not all contemporary conservatives are enthusiastic about this federalist revolution. Indeed one of them, John T. Noonan, Jr., who serves on the U.S. Court of Appeals for the Ninth Circuit, finds them frightening. Noonan argues that cases such as *Boerne* and *Lopez* "do not depend on any words in the constitution" and "are boldly innovative." And the idea that states have sufficient sovereignty as to be immune from redress from their citizens strikes him as part of "an explosive package disturbing the ascendancy of the nation over its parts."[38] Like Gertrude Himmelfarb's unease with *First Things*, Harry Jaffa's defense of Lincoln, and William Bennett's antipathy toward M. E. Bradford, Noonan's criticisms of the Rehnquist Court suggest that not all contemporary conservatives have set themselves up in opposition to the requirements for American greatness. Still, Noonan's is a voice of dissent, barely able to make itself heard in conservative precincts thrilled with the possibility of returning the law of the land to where it was in the 1880s.

Noonan's frustration is due to the fact that the national authority federalists seek to limit what was never firmly established to begin with. Even as late as the twenty-first century, as political scientist Sidney M. Milkis has written, "our current politics does not confidently presume the existence of a national state."[39] The American nation-state is big enough to tax people in noticeable ways and to influence how they act, but it is also handicapped enough in function and sufficiently starved of funding not to be able to deliver public goods either efficiently or universally. In Europe, big government creates constituencies for bigger government. In America, a national state that is never quite big enough fuels endless advocacy to make it smaller. This is the environment in which contemporary federalism flourishes. When government fails, as in many ways it is often preprogrammed to do, the only solutions are to expand it and to give it even more power or to limit it and put the power somewhere else. There may not be anything specifically Southern about the appeal of those who take the latter course, but that is only because the South's local opposition to strong government has, ironically perhaps, been nationalized.

There are good grounds for debating whether New Deal–style economic regulation went too far or whether the U.S. Supreme Court was too zealous in its attempts to apply the Fourteenth Amendment to the states; reasonable people can disagree over those issues and still be committed to the idea of American greatness. But something more than political disagreement is at stake in these new federalism cases. In the more ill-considered comments coming from the conservative end of the U.S. Supreme Court, one hears language that calls not only the New Deal into question but the entire establishment of American national sovereignty. In 1995, for example, in a case involving term limits, Justice Clarence Thomas wrote that

"The ultimate source of the Constitution's authority is the consent of the people of each individual State, not the consent of the undifferentiated people of the Nation as a whole,"[40] as if Marshall had never lived, Calhoun had never died, and the Civil War had never been fought. We must presume that Thomas, who believes so strongly in the binding power of words, chose his words very carefully, and, if so, one can hardly imagine words more destructive of the American idea of greatness. For Thomas is not suggesting that Americans ought to have a debate between different ways of achieving national greatness. He is instead calling the idea of nationhood itself into question, no matter how many years were given—nor how many lives were taken—in establishing its ability to act in the name of all.

〜 As Justice Thomas's remark suggests, John Noonan may actually be underestimating how truly radical the ideas of contemporary conservatives actually are. Noonan is concerned that in the name of federalism, states will come to possess sovereign immunity at the expense of the nation. Yet to libertarians, who form yet one more part of the contemporary conservative intellectual agenda, any kind of sovereignty, state or national, constitutes an interference with the freedom-of-business enterprise. It is not state sovereignty they seek but a more favorable business climate; as Michael Greve of the American Enterprise Institute puts it, the aim of his form of Federalism is not, as was the case when advocates of states' rights dominated the debate, just to limit the power of the federal government. Greve has economic as well as political objectives; he wants to encourage states to compete with one another to attract business by lowering the costs they impose upon its activities.[41] Libertarians like him, although they call themselves Federalist, are not really a party to the long-standing debate between Federalists and anti-Federalists. Their goal is to weaken the capacities of all forms of government wherever they can be found, whether in Richmond or Washington. National greatness simply never enters into their calculations because, their focus so exclusively on markets, there is, and ought not to be, any national society capable of becoming great.

Libertarianism was just a half-century ago an obscure trend within those constellations of ideas and movements generally labeled conservative. Its intellectual founders, Freidrich von Hayek and Ludwig von Mises, were far outside the mainstream of American economic thought, and even though these thinkers found a disciple in Milton Friedman, pure laissez-faire economics remained for some time an intellectual exercise rather than a guide to policy. Libertarianism's political problem was that it had no constituency. It spoke, it believed, on behalf of business, but business, comfortable with a large and regulative state, did not want to hear its message. When Richard Nixon became president, his economic program was as far from libertarian as one could imagine, including, as it did, the anathema of wage and price controls. In his own way, Nixon had ambitious visions for the United States, and he likely understood that those advocating unrestricted freedom for business to conduct its affairs would not be compatible with the idea of a strong state.

Ronald Reagan was more comfortable with libertarian themes than Richard Nixon, especially in his attraction to a form of "supply-side economics" that would permit tax cutting without, or so the administration's economists insisted, crimping economic growth. But, as libertarians knew, and as Reagan's budget director David Stockman later acknowledged, the real objective of the Reagan tax cut was "a frontal assault on the welfare state."[42] If that was indeed the objective, there is little doubt that, in the end, it failed. As critics of supply-side economics warned, tax cuts led to budget deficits that slowed growth and increased inflation. Reagan, in addition, lacked the true zeal necessary to reverse programs that, however easily denounced by conservatives, were still popular among those who benefited from them. Libertarians thought they had a winner in Reagan, but he proved to be a disappointment.

Although libertarians expressed their disappointment with Reagan by running a candidate—Ron Paul, a Republican congressman from Texas—against him in 1984, they had one more chance to influence the Republican Party. Libertarian-oriented Texans such as Dick Armey and Tom DeLay, unlike Paul, decided to commit to the party and to push it in a libertarian direction. Their task was facilitated by the fact that libertarian ideas began to develop during the 1980s a political constituency they never before had. Part of that constituency came from the energy that conservative political activists, motivated by a hatred of the income tax and hostility toward government regulation, brought to the Republicans in the South and West. Another part came from businessmen once willing to accept government regulation, who, in a more competitive economic environment, saw in deregulation an opportunity to cut costs. Cultural libertarianism made its presence felt among those who may have preferred strong environmental and regulatory controls on business but who did not want their sexual lives regulated or their privacy curtailed. As the intellectual tide turned against the idea of a regulated economy—it was a Democrat, Bill Clinton, who proclaimed that the era of big government was over—libertarianism, once an intellectual movement supported by aging émigrés, found itself appealing to the young and relying on cutting-edge theories borrowed from evolutionary biology and artificial intelligence to buttress its claims.[43]

Before long, groups with different perspectives but with similar complaints about government intrusion found themselves informally forming what conservative activist Grover Norquist calls the "Leave Us Alone coalition."[44] Michael Greve describes its members as including "gun owners, school choice and home schooling groups, the term limits movement, property rights groups, religious advocacy and lay organizations, tax limitation groups, small business owners, and so on." It is as if all those in the United States who had reason to be fearful of the exercise of national authority found each other irrespective of their cause or even of their political leanings. Libertarians now had a constituency, indeed a host of constituencies. Their arrival on the political stage seemed assured, especially when Republicans attracted to their agenda, including Speaker of the House Newt Gingrich, assumed power in 1994 and signed on to the libertarian-inspired Contract with America.

Heady with success, libertarians began to see themselves as key players in contemporary conservative politics. Greve, for example, insists that groups such as the "Leave Us Alone" coalition can play the same role in ensuring that the Supreme Court carries forward its Federalist agenda that liberal and civil rights groups played in hewing the Court to its national program.

The Court, Greve points out, "cannot unilaterally impose its will on the country." But it can search "for constituencies that will support Federalism and provide the Court with room for greater advances somewhere down the road," including those who "are fiercely antinationalist and anti-elitist."[45] His remarks are suggestive of the transformation undergone by American conservatism. Unlike the conservatives of the Federalist period, who were antidemocratic in spirit and nationalist in aspiration, today's conservatism, touched by libertarianism, is populist in appeal and localist at heart. This is a conservatism, not of ambition, but of resignation. Its solution to the often complicated question of how best the state might embody the ideal of the nation is to do away with the state no matter what happens to the nation.

Of course libertarians will insist that their objective is not to weaken the nation but to strengthen it by unleashing the power of private enterprise. But leaving aside the obvious fact that global enterprises increasingly act as if they have no nation, pure laissez-faire is a recipe for national weakness. No nation can be great without strong industrial performance. But nor can a nation that insists that everything be measured by market freedom. Greatness, which has always been the exception rather than the rule in the American experience, must be willed into being over the objections of all those forces that benefit from the individualistic culture, decentralized political structures, and profit-seeking opportunities that dominate everyday American life. Yet willing something into existence is precisely what libertarianism most opposes; order, in the libertarian view of the world, should emerge spontaneously out of the uncoordinated actions of individuals. National greatness, to a libertarian's ears, sounds suspiciously like national planning, and indeed all the advocates of American greatness from Alexander Hamilton to Roosevelt's brain trust were the planners of their day. Like original intent, libertarianism operates as a prior restraint on any temptation we might have to direct our collective actions along self-chosen paths.

Libertarianism's preference for small government found a warm reception with George W. Bush, who has been determined to reward antigovernment forces with their prized, and long-sought, objective: a tax cut. Rarely, in fact, has American politics witnessed anything as striking as the determination of the president to get that tax cut—actually, a series of them— passed, no matter how much the economy, the world situation, and his rationales for them changed. Mr. Bush is the first Republican president to make libertarianism the centerpiece of his presidency, and unless a future Congress engages in the unlikely action of repealing or refusing to extend the tax cuts when they expire, the United States is unlikely to possess for decades the financial wherewithal to achieve any of the objectives its leaders set out to realize.

As libertarians quickly began to realize, however, George W. Bush is with them only on the revenue side; when it comes to the expenditures provided by government, he is a big spender, indeed one of the biggest spenders of recent times. In his first term in office, he vetoed none of the legislation that crossed his desk, no matter what its cost. Indeed, he combined his policy of tax cuts with support for such expensive ventures as reconstruction in Iraq, Medicare reform, and a new energy policy by pushing most of the costs associated with them on to future generations. Furthermore, despite all their talk about smaller government—politicians like Dick Armey, in the heady days of the Contract with America, talked of cutting the size of the federal government in half—Republican legislators put partisanship ahead of principle and joined in the spending frenzy unleashed by the Bush administration. ("To the victor goes the spoils," was Armey's justification for his support for budget-busting Republican programs in 2001.)[46] If libertarianism means returning the federal government to the size it had reached before the New Deal, libertarianism is dead, one reason a number of prominent libertarian intellectuals, and even an occasional Republican congressmen, found themselves severely disquieted by the Bush approach to domestic policy.[47]

Rather than rejoicing that a theory as doctrinaire as libertarianism has been consigned to the political dustbin, however, advocates of American greatness face something in the Bush presidency that might be worse than an unbending commitment to small government. Principled libertarians oppose not just liberal government but all government, including subsidies to private corporations; a perfectly libertarian world would still be an egalitarian one in the sense that everyone would be equally prevented from relying on government to improve his or her condition in life.

What has emerged in Washington under Mr. Bush, by contrast, is a system by which those who need government least obtain, through their campaign contributions, its greatest support, while those with few resources face a competitive free market that richly subsidized corporations manage to avoid. This is a system with all of libertarian's disadvantages without any of its benefits. Government, in the Bush administration's vision of America, is to be prevented from establishing the direction society needed to take to realize its ideals; if anything, government is to be even more hobbled in this effort than it would have been under laissez-faire for not only would it have to overcome an inactive state to realize the national interest, it would also need to confront the entrenched powers of those able to use government to reinforce their privileges. Yet none of this is to be carried out with even a hint of equality, for while the powerful will benefit from governmental expenditure, ordinary Americans will suffer the consequences of government's lack of revenue. Libertarianism for the powerless only is not exactly what principled advocates for the free market had in mind in the days when laissez-faire seemed a hopeless utopia, but it is what the Republican majority in Washington is trying to bring into existence. Of all the items on Mr. Bush's agenda for his second term, none seems as unshakable as his commitment to making permanent the tax cuts he achieved during his first term, a decision bound to leave behind one America blessed by governmental largesse and another (and larger one) harmed by public indifference.

⌒— America's greatest libertarian was William Graham Sumner, whose classic work, *What Social Classes Owe Each Other*, provided a succinct introduction to what has come to be called Social Darwinism in American life. Although widely identified as a conservative, which he surely was, Sumner wanted no part in the foreign policy adventures of his time. Opposed to Teddy Roosevelt's plans for military preparedness, Sumner agreed with those, like Missouri Senator Carl Schurz, who formed the Anti-Imperialist League. For Sumner, free market advocacy and foreign policy isolationism went hand in hand.[48] Although the major attraction of anti-imperialism for him was economic, talk of war also meant talk of sacrifice, as if, contrary to his most crucial beliefs, social classes owed one another something after all.

Contemporary libertarians share Sumner's anti-imperialist proclivities. "Wartime," writes libertarian thinker David Boaz, "has occasioned such extensions of state power as conscription, the income tax, tax withholding, wage and price controls, rent control, censorship, crackdowns on dissent, and Prohibition, which really began with a 1917 statute." War, it is true, "threatens the survival of the society" and for that reason, libertarians will put up with it when necessary. But, Boaz continues, "then, after the emergency passes, the government neglects to give up the power it has seized, the courts agree that a precedent has been set, and the state settles comfortably into its new, larger domain."[49] No wonder libertarians such as James Brovard, whose best-selling books made one of the strongest contemporary cases against government, attacked President George W. Bush's war against Saddam Hussein as an attempt "to cajole Americans into acquiescing to a preemptive attack against a nation that posed no threat to the United States," an analysis little different in tone or substance than one hears from the left end of the political spectrum.[50] Libertarians like Boaz and Brovard take their inspiration, not from generals and statesmen, but from antiwar writers such as Randolph Bourne. Either that or, like Charles Murray, they write books with titles like *What It Means to Be a Libertarian* and manage to avoid the awkward question of national defense entirely.[51]

When applied to domestic policy, libertarianism carries with it tax cuts and restraints on government spending designed to leave government too small to undertake anything ambitious.

When applied to foreign policy, libertarianism serves as a reminder of the well-established link in American political thought and practice between conservatism and isolationism. Although in the early years of the twenty-first century, the term "anti-imperialist" conjures up people attracted to the left, historically anti-imperialism has found its home among those who believed in the supremacy of markets, opposed government's ability to engage in social reform, viewed immigration as a plot to undermine American values, insisted on the Christian character of the United States, and resented the cosmopolitan outlook they associated with decadent Europeans, especially the British.

Throughout much of the twentieth century, isolationism was not just a minor irritant within the Republican Party but was expressive of its core values. The man widely admired as "Mr. Republican," Robert A. Taft of Ohio, was isolationism's leading voice throughout the 1940s. In a bitter intraparty struggle Taft would lose the contest for the 1952 Republican nomination to Eisenhower, but even Eisenhower's assumption to the presidency did not quell isolationist sentiment within his party. Ohio's junior senator, John Bricker, had introduced an amendment in February 1952 that would have required Congressional approval of treaties and was a not very subtle attack on the World War II summits at Yalta and Potsdam. The defeat of the Bricker Amendment, urged by Eisenhower and his secretary of state John Foster Dulles, seemed to bring the Republican Party into the modern world. Within fifteen years of its introduction, Republican isolationism—and Republican isolationists—no longer had influence within the national leadership of the party. Richard Nixon, Ronald Reagan, and the two George Bushes were all presidents who deployed

American power abroad while facing little or no opposition within their own party by doing so.

Yet isolationism has conservative and Republican roots too strong to be destroyed by contemporary global realities. Under Republican presidents, conservative isolationism never really disappeared but merely changed its form. The objection of isolationists was not to foreign entanglements per se but to the American lives lost and dollars spent accompanying them. One way to pursue an active foreign policy while limiting the fiscal and bodily damage was by building up America's military capacity and then using it only when its overwhelming superiority all but guaranteed victory. Traditional military spending, like the form unleashed during World War II, was both a form of Keynesian demand-side management and a source of welfare-state-like expenditure in hospitals, troop training, and planning, and for both reasons one of its consequences was to promote both greater equality and a stronger nation state. By contrast, "Fortress America" approaches to defense would enable American power to be utilized when absolutely necessary without resulting in nation-building, either abroad or at home, and with none of the promises of social mobility that accompany it.

This form of quasi-isolationist military strategy, and not the Cold War liberalism of the 1960s and 1970s, appeals to contemporary Republican presidents. Reagan's secretary of defense Caspar Weinberger gave his name to a doctrine that imposed six conditions on the use of force abroad, including an overwhelming commitment to victory, strong domestic support, limited objectives, and other conditions designed to avoid unsustainable commitments. Colin Powell, who served as Reagan's national security advisor before becoming chairman of the Joint Chiefs of Staff and eventually secretary of state in the second Bush administration, held similar views. Partisan politics being what it is, Republican isolationism was relatively muted when Republicans were in power but came into full light during a Democratic presidency; Bill Clinton's often halfhearted efforts at humanitarian intervention in the Balkans and other regions were typically greeted by Republican politicians with hostility. Were a Democrat once again to become President, admittedly a difficult prospect to realize in the wake of John F. Kerry's defeat in 2004, there can be little doubt that Republican congressmen, who strongly supported their own president's foreign policy interventionism in Afghanistan and Iraq, would question any military actions he might undertake, no matter how strong the argument that they were necessary for global stability or the advancement of democracy and human rights. Republican politicians do not win points in Alabama or Idaho by their willingness to spend the tax money of their constituents to bring order to places about which their constituents manifest so little interest.

Among conservatives, isolationist sentiment outside the Republican Party is stronger than it is inside. Its most representative formulation can be found in the writings of Patrick Buchanan, the star of the 1992 Republican convention, but a thinker and writer whose conservatism now flourishes at the margins of the American political establishment. Buchanan, a close student of American history, cannot resist the temptation to return to the kind of anticosmopolitan, conspiratorial, obliquely anti-Semitic, and decidedly ugly style of 1940s and 1950s conservatism. Buchanan has positive words on behalf of the America First Committee, Charles A. Lindbergh, and others who ventured into apologetics for Hitler. ("Most America

Firsters," he writes, accurately if irrelevantly, "were actually small-government Republicans.") And he has negative words about Franklin Delano Roosevelt, who, with his advisors, "smeared, persecuted, and blacklisted antiwar leaders and maneuvered us into one collision after another with Germany and Japan so that war would be 'thrust upon us.' "[52] Buchanan's is the language of suspicion and betrayal, in which all political decisions with which he disagrees, such as commitments to free trade, are not the product of reasonable deductions about what is best for the country but represent instead a "betrayal" or a "sellout" by leaders more interested in pleasing other capitalists around the globe than in honoring their own country's traditions.[53] As Buchanan understands his history, the fact that Alexander Hamilton and Abraham Lincoln were protectionists means that conservatives should be projectionist now. The fact that the world changed in the meantime, and that what might be best for America could also have changed, never enters into his thinking.

It is true that America's working class, whose needs seem to have disappeared from the programs of the contemporary Republican Party, figures prominently in Buchanan's view of the world. His isolationism is very much populistic in tone, focused as it is on the need to protect jobs through high tariffs. This too is in continuity with America's past, for even though populists attacked the rich and promoted social reform, they were "ambivalent" about a strong national government—the characterization is Michael Kazin's—and were more likely to see in state-builders a Hamiltonian tendency to use government on behalf of the already well-off.[54] Isolationism and populism were frequently combined, and between them constituted two of the most powerful forces working in favor of a less powerful America. In inheriting both of them, Buchanan, were he to have any of the influence he so conspicuously lacks, would return the United States to a time when the income tax did not exist—Buchanan favors its abolition—because, except for protecting industries, government would not have all that much to do.

Other conservatives more responsible than Patrick Buchanan have also found themselves in recent years anti-imperialists at heart. Andrew Bacevich is one of the most interesting. A former military officer turned professor of international relations, Bacevich writes without the venom of Buchanan, but his actual views about American foreign policy share much with the former Republican candidate for president. For Bacevich, the end of the Cold War has seduced the American foreign policy establishment into believing that globalization is the wave of the future and that the American military ought to be used on behalf of protecting America's hegemonic position in the new globalist order. Unlike many other writers on American foreign policy, Bacevich does not believe that the administration of George W. Bush represents a radical break with previous presidents. On the contrary, there exists in his view a bipartisan commitment in Washington to a new imperial order. In his writings, Bacevich reflects a traditional military disdain for adventurism; the role of the armed forces is not to protect economic interests but to defend the country on those rare, but important, occasions when its security requires a military defense. His is a quintessentially conservative suspicion of overweening ambition. Empire is a bad thing because it requires more from America in terms of commitments—and, inevitably, finances—than America can properly give.

Americans like to believe that their greatness is not something they chose but something that history chose for them. For Bacevich, this is a myth; there is nothing reluctant in the

way we became a superpower, for this is something that we—
or at least the architects of our imperial posture—very much
wanted to do. Expressed in this fashion, there are no discernible
differences between Bacevich's criticisms of America's imperial
overreach and traditional American isolationism. Indeed, Bacevich, a conservative, is open-minded enough to appreciate
isolationist sentiments wherever he finds them, even among
thinkers widely identified with the left. Charles Beard, Bacevich recognizes, was wrong to have opposed FDR's plans to
oppose Hitler, but "although he had missed one large truth,
Beard had hit upon others," especially his understanding of the
way powerful economic interests shape foreign policy to reflect
their own needs. Bacevich even has positive things to say about
the doyen of American radical historians, William Appleman
Williams, who also made one big mistake—not recognizing
the evils of the Soviet Union—but who was right to understand
how commitments to global capitalism shape American foreign
policy. Bacevich and Williams—once again demonstrating a
crossing of ideological lines—share the idea that a simpler
America was a better one. "Williams," Bacevich correctly
points out, "yearned to recover the remembered—or idealized—life of a small boy growing up in the American heart-
land, watched over by hardworking plain folk, who were neither corrupted by great wealth nor afflicted with extreme
poverty."[55] He may have been considered by many a leftist, but
Williams actually had a great deal in common with defenders
of the South like M. E. Bradford, even if it was rural Iowa,
and not some Southern arcadia he worshiped. No wonder that,
advocate of goodness over greatness that he was, William
Appleman Williams distrusted Lincoln's antislavery platform,

which he interpreted as an opportunity to force a laissez-faire capitalist system on the United States.

A presidency like the one of George W. Bush, which talks proudly of such Wilsonian objectives as bringing democracy to the Middle East, is obviously one that has broken with the Republican Party's isolationist past. But the last word on this matter has not yet been uttered. Dreams of empire have been all too infrequent in the Republican Party; most of the neoconservatives active in the Bush administration once worked for *Democratic* Senators such as Henry "Scoop" Jackson and Daniel Patrick Moynihan. The existence of significant resistance in Iraq, which imposed greater than expected costs in both lives and funds, has exacerbated the disagreements between neoconservative believers in national greatness, who aspire to a Republican Party that has its links with Theodore Roosevelt, and libertarians and isolationists. With the war in Iraq resulting in chaos, it may well be the neoconservatives—many of whom, unlike most Republicans, were once socialists and remain Jews—who could find themselves as unwelcome in the party as patrician moderates like Mr. Bush's father.[56] Isolationism is not dead; if anything, with the Republican Party now responsible for the chaos in Iraq, it is likely to revive. So, it seems reasonable to believe, will be the temptations among our more conservative party to shy away from the kind of commitments that led William Graham Sumner to oppose so strongly the imperial ambitions of Theodore Roosevelt.

⌐ Charles Colson, former special advisor to President Nixon and convicted Watergate felon, is now a devout evangelical widely admired for his Prison Fellowship Ministries. Like Robert Bork, he is also a man so concerned about the lack of goodness in his country that he joined the *First Things* symposium questioning the legitimacy of the American regime, in his case on explicitly religious grounds. Christians, Colson points out, have never had consistent positions on the duties believers owe to their government; John Calvin, for example, was disposed toward the view that Christians owed obedience even to tyrants, while John Knox argued that on occasion—for example, when Catholics took power in his native Scotland—rebellion, even revolution could be justified. Colson is hopeful that despite America's slide toward secular hedonism, "open rebellion" can be avoided. But he also worries that this may not be possible. It is not the duty of individual Christians to resist an illegitimate state, he points out, for "only the Church collectively can decide at what point a government becomes sufficiently corrupt that a believer must resist it." Such a day of judgment may soon be upon us. "With fear and trembling, I have begun to believe that, however Christians in America gather to reach their consensus, we are fast approaching this point." If America continues on its present path, believers may have to choose between God and country, and for the truly devout, that will not be much of a choice at all.[57]

Much has been written about the rise of the religious right in American politics over the past three decades; without the contribution of Bible believers, conservatism in America would still be a minority movement. Far less attention, however, has been paid to the question of whether religious faith can come into conflict with the requirements of American greatness. There are good reasons nonetheless why the question ought to be raised. As Colson's remarks suggest, at least some believers can come to view themselves, in the phrase of theologian Stanley Hauerwas, as "resident aliens" in an otherwise hostile society.[58] Other forms of religious faith, most prominently Catholicism, are explicitly universal and throughout history have developed their own legal codes, ethical beliefs, and authoritative hierarchies that can, and sometimes do, conflict with what nation-states demand. Still others, including minority religions such as the Mennonites (who influenced Hauerwas through the writings of John Howard Yoder), have pacifist histories and tend to be wary of any of the nation-states in which their members happen to live. There is no such principled commitment to pacifism in the Jewish and most mainline Protestant traditions, but both also contain prophetic voices demanding that the actions of human beings be judged in the light of God's moral teachings—and which hold that worshiping the nation the way one worships God is a form of idolatry. When America chose not to establish a religion, it also allowed religions the freedom to find their own path independent of the state, thereby absolving any one faith of the temptation to tailor its teachings to the needs of the regime that protects it. Given a long history of distinguishing between what properly belongs to Caesar and what to Christ, there is no necessary reason why Christians, who remain the majority of America's believers, should devote the bulk of their activity to building a great society on this earth, especially when a greater kingdom awaits elsewhere.

Yet American religious believers in general, and American Christians in particular, have made patriotism central to their concerns. A persistent view of Christians since the days of the

Puritans held that God had called upon this people as a divine nation to carry out his work. Linking their quasi-Calvinist sense of American destiny with an evangelical zeal to spread the word of the Lord, American Protestants throughout much of the nineteenth century blessed America's rise to globalism, none more so than Josiah Strong, whose influential book *Our Country* (the century's second great best-seller after *Uncle Tom's Cabin*) had a strong influence on the imperial ambitions of Theodore Roosevelt.[59] Global ambitions, moreover, were frequently combined with domestic ones; a substantial number of influential Christian thinkers a century or so ago found themselves appalled by William Graham Sumner's Social Darwinism, as well as by his atheism, and began to formulate, in explicitly religious terms, the need for a welfare state that would help realize the goals of Christian charity at home. One sees all these trends combined in the figure of Walter Rauschenbusch, well known for his advocacy of the Social Gospel, but a man who, for all his later criticism of World War I, was an unabashed supporter of the Spanish-American War, his language in its defense as marred by racism as any other imperialist of his time.[60]

America's contemporary conservative movement has a strong religious component, especially among evangelical Protestants who have turned away from their previous uninvolvement with politics to become core supporters of the Republican Party. Like earlier figures in American religious history, including those of far more liberal outlook, they share the belief that America has been chosen by God to do great things. One finds in their sermons little of Christ's teachings about turning the other cheek and more of the kind of muscular Christianity that leads to strong support for America's military missions wherever and whenever they occur. They are, for reasons of theology, especially taken with the importance of having an American foreign policy capable of coming to the defense of the State of Israel, which in turn has led them to support strong foreign policy actions in the Middle East. First communism, which was explicitly antireligious, and then Islam, which many of them view as anti-Christian, furnished exactly the kinds of enemies that fit their conception of why a strong American national defense is necessary. Their churches are the ones most likely to provide the troops who fight in countries like Afghanistan and Iraq. For all these reasons and more, the religious right is not, at first glance, an enemy of American greatness the way other elements of the contemporary conservative coalition are.

But first glances are often deceiving, and especially so in this case. While ordinary evangelicals have been as strongly influenced by the culture of modernity as other Americans, the leadership of the politically active religious right—men such as Jerry Falwell, Gary Bauer, and Pat Robertson—advocates extremist positions that often have little to do with the worldly lives of those for whom they presume to speak. Those positions, as it happens, also reveal attitudes that stand in bitter opposition to the idea that America can aspire to the greatness for which its most inspiring leaders had hoped.

Conservative Christians activists are not children of the Enlightenment who identify progress as good and identify America as synonymous with progress. They have in their midst no Benjamin Franklin curious to the point of inventiveness about the natural world, no Thomas Jefferson intent on founding a great university, no Gifford Pinchot–like conservationists determined to bring scientific management to natural resources, and no Rexford Tugwells who believe that people's fates should not be held hostage to the whims of unregulated markets. On the contrary, evangelical activists emerged out of a fundamentalist movement that saw in modernity ways of thinking and acting incompatible with faith and that dedicated itself to resisting those intellectual developments that enabled the United States to assume global leadership in science and technology.

Evangelical elites these days have left behind much of their fundamentalist heritage, but they continue to cast wary eyes on scientific and technological innovation. The best example is provided, not by birth control and abortion, which involve clear-cut moral differences over which people can and will disagree, but the use of embryonic stem cells for medical research, a morally murkier and also potentially life-saving technology that has won the support of a number of prominent conservatives, including Senator Orrin Hatch of Utah and former first lady Nancy Reagan. Conservative Christian activists nonetheless remain strongly opposed to research involving embryonic stem cells. Their opposition was strong enough to influence President Bush's decision to restrict federal funding to already-existing stem cell lines. Not even Ronald Reagan's death, after suffering from a disease that stem cell research could possibly have helped cure, changed the national political dynamics on this issue.

Some may believe that conservative Christians should be praised for their adherence to principle, and it is certainly true that neither considerations of scientific progress nor the prospect of losing an economic advantage to other countries swayed the opponents of stem cell research. Yet adherence to principle has never been as important to ideas of American greatness as pragmatic flexibility, a historical lesson strongly reaffirmed in this case. For it was not only their opposition to stem cell research but the way they opposed it that suggested how far removed conservative Christian activists were from the constellation of attitudes and practices associated with American greatness. Conservative Christian leaders played a relatively small role in the debates over whether therapeutic cloning existed on a different moral plane than odious forms of human cloning and never responded to Senator Hatch's view that those who are pro-life ought to be sympathetic to the relief of human suffering; they opposed, in other words, not only the science, but the worldview of reasoned discussion that accompanies modern science. No wonder that President Bush's actions in this area, such as his administration's frequent interference with scientific peer review in order to satisfy ideological correctness, strikes so many as morally and politically small-minded, guided, as it is, by an effort to please a constituency willing to draw the line against progress far more tightly than has been customary in American life.

Social science has been as important to the quest for American greatness as natural science, especially throughout the twentieth century when overcoming depression and fighting wars across the globe demanded extensive coordination, planning, and intelligence. Yet Christian conservatives, who had strong reservations about natural science, were equally hostile to social science, especially the kind they associated with the New Deal and World War II. Throughout the twentieth century, Christian conservative leadership remained stubbornly libertarian; it existed in the shadow of J. Gresham Machen, an

important fundamentalist intellectual and vehement opponent of all government, and not in the shadow of Walter
Rauschenbusch, Josiah Strong, or, perhaps most appropriately,
Richard T. Ely, the founder of the American Economics Association, a prominent social reformer, and a devout Christian
believer. Even today, the outlook of Machen's evangelical descendents possesses little or no confidence that a strong society
can be built through deliberate human action; instead, it is
clouded by a suspicion of human endeavor that precludes hope
of social improvement through political means. Aware that
their distaste for government could be taken by their critics as
evidence for a lack of Christian charity, conservative Christian
intellectuals and politicians have increasingly made the case
for compassion based on private charity.[61] But even if such
efforts could supplant government and do a better job of im-
proving the conditions of the poor—there is scant evidence,
by the way, that they ever could—there still remain among
most conservative Christian political activists an unhappiness
with the whole idea that income inequality or poverty are not
evidence of our sinful conduct but instead conditions that can
be ameliorated through the deliberate decisions made by a political community.

Something far more important than their positions on social
security or stem cell research also stands in the way of an identification with a strong American nation among the leaders of
the religious right. The United States "is the greatest nation on
the face of God's earth," the Rev. Jerry Falwell once said. "I
love this country, I love every square foot of this land."[62] Yet
Falwell is the heir to a tradition of apocalyptic thinking that
holds that God's judgment is about to descend on all nations,

including ones like the United States, which he has for so long favored. "Uncle Sam, with all his might, will be no match for Antichrist," wrote the editor of *Christian Digest* in 1942. His, more than Falwell's, has been the widely accepted view among fundamentalist Protestant thinkers throughout the twentieth century. "It is quite possible that Ezekiel was referring to the U.S. in part when he said: 'I will send fire—upon those who dwell securely in the coastlands,' " Hal Lindsey observed in his phenomenal 1970 best-seller *The Late Great Planet Earth.* "The forecast for the USA is gloomy," as a pseudonymous writer expressed the point in 1982. "The USA will survive, but it would appear that very few people will be left alive. Does this mean that nearly all of our 230,000,000 people will be killed? It would appear so."[63]

Such apocalyptic visions have never lost their popularity in the United States. Lindsey's book has been replaced on the best-seller lists by the "Left Behind" series, written by Tim La-Haye and Jerry B. Jenkins, which popularizes the arcane Christian theology known as premillennialism; all too briefly put, a remnant of right-thinking Christians battle the Antichrist to prepare the way for Christ's second coming.[64] Other conservative Christians find themselves attracted to a movement called Reconstructionism whose aim, media critic Mark Crispin Miller writes, "is to undo the framers' work, and force an alien form of government on the United States." [65] The influence of these ideas and movements can easily be exaggerated, as Miller's rather overheated interpretation suggests; Reconstructionism is sufficiently right wing to have been denounced by many American evangelical leaders. Still, there is little doubting that Falwell and similarly inclined fundamentalists find much of value in an atmosphere conducive to thinking more about the end times than to sharing the good news of present times.

Combining an apocalyptic sensibility with a faith in the United States as a great nation is no easy task. Falwell nonetheless tried his best. "If God is on our side, no matter how militarily superior the Soviet Union is, they could never touch us," as he once put it.[66] But surely God could not grant such a dispensation if, when looking at the country he was inclined to protect, he saw what Robert Bork and Jerry Falwell see: atheists, liberals, abortion-seeking women, and homosexuals. As much as conservative Christian activists claim to love America, they have serious problems with Americans, whose sexual conduct, dress codes, use of language, viewing habits, and indifference to sin drive them to distraction. Falwell cannot quite make up his mind whether America is doomed because of its moral decrepitude or is the savior of mankind due to its principles and power, hard as it may be to be both at the same time. His dilemma is acute: If America is great, it does not need God. But if it needs God, it cannot, at least until it finds him, be great.

Only one path exists for Falwell to resolve this contradiction, and it is not dissimilar to the one followed by Calhoun. Falwell's nationalism is contingent; for all its zeal, it comes with conditions. "We teach patriotism . . . as being synonymous with Christianity,"[67] as Falwell once put it; his great America is an America only for some, not just those who are nominal Christians, but only those who, by being born again, are real Christians. As with libertarians and federalists of even the most secular convictions, there is among conservative Christians a determined effort to condemn the actual reality of what America has become and to substitute in its place an idealized and romantic fantasy about the good society that the United States ought to be. The American greatness for which he stands aims to make great an America that has never actually existed.

Politics takes place before the Apocalypse; the days in which we live may (or may not) be the last days, but they are the only ones we have available to us to make the decisions that determine the future of our society. In real time, the influence of conservative Christian thinkers and writers on American greatness has, despite their self-asserted patriotism, been minimal, if not negative. You do not make America great by dividing it into parts and then proclaiming only some of the parts worth saving. Judging foreign policy actions by the degree to which Christians and only Christians are protected from persecution is a far cry from the dispassionate realism that great societies require for their overseas commitments. Holding out as a model for the future the predominantly monoreligious society that America was in the past hardly prepares a society to incorporate the energy provided by new immigrants in ways conducive to the nation's future. Insisting that advances in science and technology that show great promise to improve the human condition be subject to a religious veto does not allow a society either the promise of hope or an effective strategy for responding to other societies more willing to explore and discover. Were they to find the political influence they seek, conservative Christians might be able to make America good—although that, truth be told, is highly doubtful—but they could never make it great.

⌒— In the election of 2000 that brought George W. Bush to power, there was one candidate who seemed ambiguously to evoke the ideal of American greatness, in his war record, his character, his outspokenness, and his self-confidence. John McCain, to many observers, seemed as close a reimbodiment of Theodore Roosevelt as one could imagine. His efforts to win the Republican nomination for president attracted the attention of the "national greatness" intellectuals identified with magazines such as the *Weekly Standard*, who saw in him the possibility of a conservatism that would reject the isolationism, libertarianism, and suspicious xenophobia that has so often characterized the American right.

McCain's candidacy, however, could not survive the politics of the Republican Party's nomination procedure. Instead of a war hero with an enviable national record, the party turned instead to a relatively inexperienced, awkwardly inarticulate, and remarkably incurious one-term governor. As the 2000 campaign developed, it became obvious that McCain's refusal to pay homage to the conservative movement's pieties doomed his candidacy. George W. Bush understood, as John McCain either did not or did not care to acknowledge, that in contemporary politics you must pander to your base. And if your base turns out to be composed of a coalition of interests with little in common except their fear of government and their anger at the direction America has taken, then talk of national greatness has to be put aside for another day. Any influence John McCain may have on the future of the United States will have to come from the sidelines.

There is more in McCain's defeat than one man's political savvy and another's refusal to kowtow. Ideas, as Richard

Weaver reminds us, really do have consequences, and when those ideas are an odd amalgam of suspicion, nostalgia, braggadocio, and contempt for those who disagree with you, the intellectual and political movement that appeals to them is unlikely to welcome as its leader someone as strong-willed as a John McCain. The party of which he happens to be a member is one that no longer stands for the kind of national ambition and sense of historic destiny he symbolizes.

True, American conservatism has shown remarkable political skill, transforming itself, between 1964 and 2004, from a movement rejected by most Americans to one capable of holding power in all three branches of the national government. But energy and excitement cannot be a substitute for the fact that conservatism's agenda of shrinking government to the point that it can be washed down the bathroom drain—the metaphor is the property of Grover Norquist—is as inappropriate to achieving America's great objectives as Thomas Jefferson's calls for the spilling of blood every decade or so. A political party committed to national greatness would not foreclose appointing the best people it can find for the judiciary by insisting instead that only those willing to take a loyalty oath to original intent need apply. Nor would it adopt as its approach to domestic policy a libertarian fidelity to tax cuts designed to tie not only its own hands but the hands of any future administration to ambitions projects for national reconstruction. One can hardly imagine a program more hostile to the idea of national greatness than a willingness to reopen the wounds of the Civil War era by trying to undermine the painfully difficult-to-achieve sovereignty of the national government. The path to national greatness requires an unapologetic defense of nation building abroad to accompany the language of national reconstruction at home, joined, in the best of cases, with the self-confidence necessary to work with other governments to ensure conditions of international stability.

None of these John McCain–like thoughts seem to play much of a role in the Republican Party as currently constituted. And that is because on nearly all the issues that matter, conservative thought has chosen the small and niggardly over the grand and ambitious. American conservatives are clear about what they do not like—something called liberalism, which, they oddly believe, still runs the United States even after conservatives have been able to control a good deal of the media and all branches of government—but they have not been forthcoming, and certainly not in any honest way, about the kind of society they hope to put in place, no doubt because, if ever candidly articulated, a vision of further privileges for the already privileged would inspire in almost no one feelings of pride and accomplishment.

National greatness conservatives still have a place at the Republican table; they were, after all, able to commit the Bush administration to the war in Iraq. But not only did national greatness conservatives sacrifice nearly all their commitments to sit at the table, their place around it remains precarious. The energy in the contemporary Republican Party belongs to men like House Majority Leader Tom DeLay, who puts his ideology and his party ahead of his country on every issue that comes across his desk. If one looks at the Congressional wing of the Republican Party, which could become the source of future presidential candidates, George W. Bush may come to be remembered as one of the more enlightened Republican politicians of the early twenty-first century. (Who, after all, could have predicted that, in contrast to Mr. Bush, both Barry Goldwater and Ronald Reagan would go down in history as moderates.) In 2004, after all, Republicans were elected to the U.S. Congress whose extreme right-wing views make Mr. Bush's ideology look soft by comparison.

The conservative tradition is an honorable one in America, and it continues to attract thinkers whose love of their country and desire to help it achieve greatness is palpable, including Gertrude Himmelfarb, Walter Berns, William Bennett, and John T. Noonan, who have been willing to criticism the extremism within their ranks. But the nation builders have lost every important battle for the soul of their movement. Political scientists Marc Landy and Sidney M. Milkis write that all of America's greatest presidents have been tutors at heart; understanding the gap between where Americans were and where they needed to be, they used the office to educate Americans to the responsibilities they had but were often reluctant to acknowledge.[68] What is true of presidents is just as true of the ideas upon which presidents draw; to be effective over the long run, those ideas need sufficient distance from public opinion polls and the insatiable needs of politicians facing the next election—in America, there is always a next election—to develop the kinds of policies and programs that can challenge and inspire as well as reward and reinforce. As it takes the personal courage of a Teddy Roosevelt or a John McCain to become a great American leader, it takes intellectual courage to propose great ideas for America, such as the courage to insist that sometimes government is necessary and the taxes to finance its activities a small price to pay for the results it can achieve or the courage to do what is right for future generations rather than what is most likely to garner votes in the very next election.

Such courage is hard to find anywhere in American politics, but especially in the quarters of the contemporary American right. From a national greatness standpoint, conservatism in America came to power too quickly and, in so doing, has had to accommodate itself to a society that values instant gratification too much, public life too little, and difficult choices not at all. Conservatism, like religion, has shaped the culture but has also been shaped by it; it is unable to hold America up to its ideals because it sacrificed the language of ideals in its quest to gain power at any price. Today's conservative movement—populistic in its resentments, lacking in introspection, dismissive of tradition—is poorly equipped to exercise any tutorial function. (If anything, it requires a public more sober in its assessments and responsible in its conduct to tutor it out of its self-destructive urges.) Whatever its political future, this is not a movement that is going to leave America stronger than it found it. Quite the contrary: the stronger American conservatism becomes, the weaker America will be.

IV LIBERALISM'S FEAR OF AMBITION

Of all the thinkers and leaders in American history, the one least likely to appeal to contemporary Americans would surely be John C. Calhoun. A would-be aristocrat, defender of slavery, and passionate advocate for a way of life history was passing by, Calhoun ought to be something of a relic, clearly—given his brilliance—of some curiosity value, but hardly a guide to contemporary life. To be sure, conservatives like Willmoore Kendall were attracted by Calhoun, and an iconoclast like Garry Wills has in turn been fascinated by Kendall, but Kendall never claimed to be fashioning a conservatism capable of governing the modern world.[1] On the contrary, he took a perverse delight in tweaking defenders of an expansive America for their unexamined, if not contradictory, assertions.

Still, the Southern slave owners for whom Calhoun spoke were increasingly a minority in rapidly industrializing nineteenth-century America, and speaking in defense of minorities has become one of the defining characteristics of contemporary liberals. It should therefore not come as a surprise that while conservatives like Harry Jaffa can question Calhoun's commitment to equality, intellectuals on the left end of the political spectrum are willing to give the man's views a second look. Calhoun became once again a subject of interest when, on April 29, 1993, Bill Clinton nominated Lani Guinier for the position of assistant attorney general for civil rights.

The controversy surrounding Guinier's nomination focused on issues of race and affirmative action, including the unfair charge that Guinier was a "quota queen." Now that the passions have cooled, it seems clear that while race was indeed central to the brouhaha, just as important was the national seminar on the structure of government that Guinier's views stimulated. Critics of those views, including President Clinton when he later withdrew her nomination, claimed that they were undemocratic. Guinier vigorously denied the accusation, but she is, if not actively hostile to democracy, then indifferent to its usual way of conducting public affairs. As with Calhoun, procedures and principles, rather than politics and persuasion, do all the work in Guinier's analysis. Although Calhoun's name does not appear in *The Tyranny of the Majority* (it does in at least one of the law review articles on which the book is based), the various voting schemes she explores—in particular "super majority" rules in legislatures that would require not only a majority vote of the whole body but also a majority of its minority members on legislation affecting the latter's interests— are a contemporary offshoot of Calhoun's concept of concurrent majorities. "*There is nothing inherent in democracy that requires majority rule*," Guinier wrote in a sentence with which Calhoun would surely agree; majority rule, in her view, is appropriate only when majorities and minorities are not locked into fixed positions that work to the latter's disadvantage.[2] When minorities need protection against the majority's tyranny, mechanisms that can block the majority's designs on them are appropriate.

Guinier's suspicion of the majority belongs to a well-established American tradition that includes the anti-Federalists, Alexis de Tocqueville, Henry David Thoreau, and twentieth-century conservatives and civil libertarians. But it is a notion that also has had little support among those whose primary objective has been the building of a great America. True, the early Federalists, aristocratic in their sentiments, were hardly advocates of democracy. But for them, as well as for the conservative nationalists that followed, majority rule may have been problematic, but minority rule was worse. America, blessed with great natural resources and a fantastic entrepreneurial spirit, was trapped in a premodern political structure. Its only hope for greatness was to find a way to limit the disproportionate amount of power of minorities, especially the one from the Old South that had been such a beneficiary of constitutional compromises that weakened the republic but won its support for union. As democracy began to offer the only prospect for overcoming their entrenched power, the fear among state builders in the North and West was that the majority had too little power, not too much.

By rejecting the notion that a strong nation requires a mature state, Guinier established herself as at heart an eighteenth-century political thinker. Power, in her view, is best exercised when most dispersed. Her framers are the ones who cited Montesquieu approvingly, not the ones who feared the political vacuum created by the Articles of Confederation; Guinier manages to interpret Alexander Hamilton, the most sympathetic of all the founders to national power, as an adherent of Lord Acton's famous dictum that power corrupts. This is not the suspicion of American nationhood that one finds in Clarence Thomas's preference for states' rights, but it is a not very distant cousin. As with conservative opponents of national sovereignty, Guinier believes that other objectives are more important to America than the capacity of government to mobilize power in defense of the national interest. Participation and fairness count more than democracy and authority in her view, and if to ensure these values we have to return to a premodern political structure, that is a price worth paying. Although expressed from the left rather than the right, Guinier's is a vision of American goodness in which more attention ought to be paid to society's soul than to its strength.

In her reflections on her failure to win support for her nomination, Guinier expressed puzzlement that liberal senators like Joseph Biden and Diane Feinstein were not on her side.[3] She should not have been so surprised. Although conservatives took the lead in criticizing Guinier, they were attacking someone whose views were not all that different from their own; two law professors, to cite just one example, in tune with a suspicion of majority rule that has in recent years characterized the conservative disposition, have called for supermajority voting rules in legislatures to prevent ordinary majorities from passing spending bills that result in either higher taxes or major deficits.[4] For liberals, by contrast, Guinier's reservations about majority rule strike at the heart of the governing strategy they have adopted throughout most of the twentieth century. Influenced by the twin experiences of the Great Depression and World War II, postwar liberals were convinced that America's eighteenth-century Constitution was inadequate to the challenges of the modern world. Neither domestic reform nor international objectives, they insisted, could be achieved unless a national liberal majority could be built sufficient to circumvent the minority fiefdoms that stood in the way of progress.

A classic work in this vein was James MacGregor Burns's *The Deadlock of Democracy*, first published in 1963. Burns, like Guinier, understood the Constitution as a Madisonian effort to let ambition check ambition, but, unlike her, he lamented the restrictions on the will of the majority inherent in a system of checks and balances. Madison's twentieth-century legacy, according to Burns, was a four-party system in which both Democrats and

Republicans were divided into presidential and congressional wings. This system allowed "flexibility, accessibility, and representativeness in our governmental system," he wrote, but at the expense of "leadership, vigor, speed, and effective and comprehensive national action." The Kennedyesque language was deliberate. Addressing his book as much to the sitting president as to his other readers, Burns argued that for the deadlock of democracy to be broken, "a congressional as well as a presidential victory in 1964" would have to take place. "The President would win so sweepingly that he would carry into Congress the kind of majorities that Roosevelt enjoyed after 1936."[5]

Should the liberal president elected in 1964 achieve such a mandate—as we all know, one did, even if his name was Johnson and not Kennedy—what, Burns asked, should he do with it? Burns devoted some attention to the unfinished business of the New Deal, but his real concern was not with substance but with procedure. The important thing was not to pass this law or that, but to reform the Madisonian political system. The United States, Burns believed, contained an inherent liberal majority, but that majority's will was frustrated by America's decentralized and fractured political universe. It was not the Republicans who blocked the efforts of liberals to realize their agenda so much as it was the leaders of the Congressional Democrats, nearly all of them from one-party states with histories of racial segregation, who used their power as committee chairmen to prevent or water down reform. The best hope to circumvent their power was through an enlargement of the electorate that would force Congress to change its ways. The reforms urged by Burns—such as creating national political parties to reduce rural overrepresentation in legislatures and relying on federal power to guarantee the voting rights of the disenfranchised—were designed to fashion a new majority capable of giving the United States the British-style political system it deserved. Burns knew that his proposals were unrealistic, but if Americans began to think more about the undemocratic legacy of their Madison system, they might be persuaded to undertake the difficult task of creating a government more appropriate to twentieth-century needs.

The contrast between Burns and Guinier is striking. Burns hoped to enlarge the suffrage, but for Guinier, "votes should not count more than voters"; she is less concerned with the qualitative question of how many vote and more with qualitative ones of who they vote for and why. Nor does Guinier seek to build a new majority; in fact she rejects coalition building entirely in favor of a model of politics in which interests are not only guaranteed representation, but are given the right to have their preferences satisfied "a fair proportion of the time." Burns thought that an enlarged majority could rely on presidential leadership to overcome Congressional inaction, whereas Guinier, like an eighteenth-century republican fearful of monarchy, writes that "the legislature, not the President, best represents the people." To pass reform legislation, Burns urged that power be concentrated, but for Guinier, who advocates collaborative rather than confrontational forms of decision-making, "centralized authority . . . may reflect a deeply felt need to preserve the control of those in power while ostensibly protecting democratic values."[6] Both *The Deadlock of Democracy* and *The Tyranny of the Majority* concern themselves with procedures, but their remedies are diametrically opposite. Burns wants rules that that will curtail minorities so that the majority can find its voice; Guinier wants reforms that will curtail the majority so that minorities can speak louder. One was an advocate for a good America that would represent all its elements fairly, the other for a great America capable of having its will enacted.

Although we no longer have a Calhoun, Burns noted at one point in his book, "antimajoritarianism is still powerful as an intellectual and emotional proposition."[7] When he wrote that, he was thinking about the political right; antimajoritarianism for him was a synonym for elitism, the view, not uncommon in the aftermath of totalitarianism, that held that ordinary people could not be trusted because they could so easily be lumped together into an irrational and undifferentiated mass. Little could Burns have foreseen how correct he was in thinking that antimajoritarianism had not yet died. Yet we also have to take note of how wrong he was in attributing such views to the right. Conservatives these days love to proclaim, in the manner of cable television host Bill O'Reilly, their identification with ordinary folk. It is thinkers on the left, if Lani Guinier is any indication, who cannot bring themselves to believe, at least with respect to racial justice, that ordinary Americans will, by their own efforts, do the right and proper thing.

In many ways, *The Deadlock of Democracy*—and similar accounts of the underperforming American system of government from writers as diverse as Maxwell Taylor and Arthur Schlesinger, Jr.—represents one of the last gasps of liberalism's commitment to the idea of national greatness.[8] The age of Burns is forward looking and optimistic, as if liberals are finally about to gather their just reward. The age of Guinier is defensive and backward looking, as if the best for which liberals can hope are changes in the rules that will protect their values the way high tariffs protect threatened manufacturers. The shift from one to the other is perhaps the strongest evidence we have of how contemporary liberalism in America has lost its nerve. Faced with an unexpected shift in public opinion and political leadership to the right in the aftermath of the 1960s and 1970s, the left, instead of standing for an ambitious program capable of realizing American greatness, has become fearful that national greatness is just a code word for rolling back the relatively few gains that it had been able to achieve in more favorable times. For a thinker such as Lani Guinier the deadlock of democracy is not a sorry state to be lamented but the best that the left can hope for in an age of conservative domination.

⌒— One could dismiss the importance of Lani Guinier's neo-Calhounianism on the grounds that she is an idiosyncratic thinker whose ideas, often presented in maddeningly obscure fashion, represent no important intellectual trend. In fact, Guinier's fear of majority rule is only one part of a revival of interest in eighteenth-century conceptions of the structure of government, and the preoccupation with goodness those conceptions entail, originating from the left end of America's political spectrum.

Consider the anti-Federalists. A half a century ago, they were described, in a famous article about them by Cecelia Kenyon, as "men of little faith." The faith of which she spoke had nothing to do with religion; Kenyon, writing very much in the same spirit (and at roughly the same time) as James MacGregor Burns, attributed to them a lack of faith in the nation. Localist in outlook and fearful of a heterogeneous society, "the last thing in the world they wanted," she wrote, "was a national democracy which would permit Congressional majorities to operate freely and without restraint."[9] Kenyon's essay was directed against Charles Beard's economic interpretation of the Constitution; she wanted to show how little sense it made, in treating the Federalists as a capitalist ruling class, to find in the anti-Federalists some kind of progressive alternative. But her essay can also be read as explaining why conservatives such as Herbert Storing found the anti-Federalists appealing; in Storing's view, they anticipated the fear that centralized authority, and the taste for huge ambition that accompanies it, would destroy the primarily rural and local communities in which, he believed, American liberty flourished.

Conservatives still tend to find the anti-Federalists attractive, but in recent years they have been joined by thinkers on the other side of the political spectrum. Influenced by the 1960s, with its emphasis on local community organizing, participatory democracy, and back-to-the-land yearnings, some writers began to see the anti-Federalists, not as political reactionaries, but as incipient populists whose ideas stand up well in comparison to the more authoritarian and elitist designs of Federalists such as Hamilton; Staughton Lynd, for example, one of the New Left's earliest activists, wrote a master's thesis sympathetic to anti-Federalism and then as a radical lawyer advocated using localist ideas such as eminent domain to prevent plant closings.[10] For others on the left, the fact that anti-Federalists opposed the Alien and Sedition Acts makes them a kind of American Civil Liberties Union avant la lettre.[11] "In a very real sense," historian Saul Cornell has written, "the Anti-Federalist ranks included both the historical antecedents of Goldwater Republicans and Students for a Democratic Society."[12] Given the suspicion toward government that emerged after the twin crises of Vietnam and Watergate, it can hardly be surprising that those who expressed hostility toward the national government in an earlier age would begin to attract considerable attention later.

The anti-Federalists, however, come with sufficiently unpleasant associations—Kenyon's description of their hostility toward what today we call diversity is hard to ignore—to make them inappropriate models for the contemporary left. The same is not true of the republicans, not the political party, I hasten to add, but the intellectual and political movement that made virtue central to its outlook on the world. Although some anti-Federalists were republicans, not all republicans were anti-Federalists; Jefferson, the most famous example, was a supporter of the Constitution and a Demo-cratic-Republican, while John Adams, who is generally included in the republican tradition, was a Federalist. Still, there were consider-able areas of overlap between the two. Republicans trusted the small and immediate over the centralized and distant. Their dislike of cities and sympathy for agricultural ways of life is well known. Fearful of standing armies, their most lasting invention was the citizen militia, from which has emerged today's National Guard. Appreciative of duties and not just asserters of rights, sensitive to the temptations of corruption, consistently upholding the ideal of disinterested service, classical republicans, as Joyce Appleby writes, offer "late-twentieth-century men and women an attractive alter-native to liberalism and socialism. . . . Like a magnet, republican-ism has drawn to it the fillings of contemporary discontents with American politics and culture. Unlike Marxism, it has done this by establishing its origins before Independence and hence establishing authentic American roots."[13]

The Republican revival has flowed from a wide variety of streams, including the historiography of J.A.G. Pocock and Gor-don Wood, the attraction to the classical polis associated with Hannah Arendt, and the centrality of a lively public square identi-fied with Jürgen Habermas. But as if to prove how correct Appleby's diagnosis is, the best known attempt to rediscover the uses of the republican tradition for contemporary politics contains the word "discontent" in its title and self-consciously chooses American history as its focus. Michael Sandel's *Democracy's Dis-content* has two objectives. One is to criticize a philosophical tradi-tion that insists that the right is prior to the good, especially as it takes the contemporary form of arguing that government must remain neutral regarding competing conceptions of the good life. The other is to show how over time American society has retreated from a republican conception of politics recognizing the need to cultivate citizens who could band together in communities to achieve the good and has replaced it with a procedural understanding of politics seeking to expand the range of choices people can make without passing judgments on the kinds of choices they do make.

Theoretically speaking, nothing in Sandel's analysis should preclude the possibility of American greatness. A strong America presumes a strong commitment to the goals for which America stands; to insist, as Lincoln did, on equal national citizenship is not to remain neutral between equality and inequality. It follows that the moral formation of citizens can be just as vital to state builders seeking to centralize power as it is to agrarian localists suspicious of national authority, so long as the former include among their objectives a concern with virtue. And as Sandel tells the story, this is precisely what happened, especially in the earlier years of the American republic. Alexander Hamilton, Sandel observes, made a case for economic growth on the grounds that "an advanced economy of commerce, manufacturing, sound currency, and public finance" could achieve "a vision of republican glory and greatness." Along similar lines, the internal improvements sought by Whigs such as Henry Clay were "moral as well as material." The Whigs, ever conscious of the need to cultivate citizens of good character, included men like Horace Mann, who devoted his public life to the public school, and Daniel Webster, who strongly supported the Sunday school movement offering religious instruction, and a day off from work, on the Sabbath.[14]

Yet as Sandel develops his thesis that a republican conception of politics was replaced by a procedural one, advocates of a less grand vision for the United States are consistently viewed as the friends of virtue and those who stood for ambitious programs and national and international expansion as its enemies. Thus we have the demise of the Knights of Labor, which emphasized the role of citizen-producers and engaged in moral reform, and its replacement by the American Federation of Labor, which accepted the wage system and sought higher pay for workers. Replaying the same script, progressives such as Louis D. Brandeis and Woodrow Wilson made little headway with their insistence on decentralized power and industrial democracy, especially in comparison to Theodore Roosevelt's New Nationalism, which accepted trusts as a necessary evil and sought to regulate their affairs.

Sandel is especially disappointed with the New Deal. After his reelection in 1936, Franklin Delano Roosevelt turned away from his more Brandeis-inspired advisors such as Felix Frankfurter to adopt a Keynesian fiscal policy designed to stimulate the economy. Keynesianism, as Sandel interprets it, put the last nail in the coffin of republicanism; aiming, unlike Hamilton's lingering concern with virtue, to achieve economic growth for its own sake, Keynesian fiscal policy assumes "that government should not form or revise, or for that matter even judge, the interests and ends its citizens espouse; rather, it should enable them to pursue these interests and ends, whatever they may be, consistent with a similar liberty for others."[15] Keynesianism is to economics what *Roe v. Wade* is to rights, neutral with respect to ends and designed to allow individuals to make choices on their own behalf. In its aftermath, it seems obvious to Sandel that the reforms of the Great Society would not seek to persuade the poor to lead better lives but would throw money at them in the hope of expanding their options.

Michael Sandel is no nostalgic communitarian longing for a return to eighteenth-century ways of life. Nor is he, like Lani Guinier, a political activist speaking on behalf of a constituency. But his work nonetheless signifies a widespread feeling on the part of liberal political thinkers that something went terribly wrong as the United States pursued a postwar politics of economic growth, federal expansion, and overseas ambition. For Sandel, the price that liberals paid for their overweening ambition was to leave a concern with goodness behind; as he succinctly puts it, "fundamentalists rush in where liberals fear to tread."[16] The political philosopher Ronald Beiner is correct, in my view, to suggest that Sandel seeks "to reorient the terms by which the contemporary American left defines itself."[17] Both for its own sake and in order to outflank the right, the left needs to make questions of character formation central to its project, and if that requires sacrificing an ambitious program of national greatness, so be it.

Sandel's message has not gone unheard in the world of real politics. While cochairing with former New Hampshire senator Warren Rudman the U.S. Commission on National Security/ Twenty-First Century, which predicted with astonishing accuracy the vulnerability of the United States to something like the September 11 attack, former senator and Democratic presidential candidate Gary Hart took time away from American politics to obtain a doctorate at Oxford University. His thesis, later published as a book, sought to establish the relevance of the republican tradition to the issues facing contemporary America. Hart believes that "Jefferson's democratic republican ideal might yield a new political culture or a polity founded upon humanity's essentially social nature; a new destiny founded on participation in community life; the restoration of a public ethic that supersedes the private, commercial self; and the elevation of the common good and of commonwealth institutions, such as public schools as instruments of civic education, community welfare as a political and moral function of the ward, and local security provided by the citizen-soldier." Ward republics at the local level will not, in his vision, replace national authority, but they can and should supplement what Washington can do. Local republics can be given more of a role in antipoverty programs and other efforts to ensure economic justice. They can improve the educational system by making schools more responsible to, and integrated with, community life. And they can even help fight terror, for it may prove to be the case that the "defense of the U.S. homeland in the early twenty-first century may depend more on the National Guard, the Constitutionally recognized militia, than on the armed might of the superpower's permanent standing military forces."[18]

Hart's proposals for ward republics illustrate the degree to which contemporary liberals feel that something in the soul of American liberalism has been lost. Welfare, growth, and security, as liberals and Democrats understood those objectives throughout most of the twentieth century, no longer seem appropriate to the problems faced by the twenty-first. By conventional political labels, Hart remains a liberal, and his commitment to the Democratic Party, and its 2004 presidential candidate John Kerry, was strong. Yet when it comes to both foreign and domestic policy, Hart's trumpet is uncertain, and his Jeffersonian language evokes the era of the Declaration of Independence more than that of the Constitution and the *Federalist Papers*. "The republican ideal proposed here," Hart writes, "is avowedly not utopian, unrealistic, or nostalgic."[19] But the fact that he has to say so betrays a lingering sense that it is indeed all those things. This is not meant to condemn his ideas, for there is nothing wrong with a little utopianism every now and then. But turning to local communities and their concern with goodness as the best way to deal with a domestic polity dominated by powerful and self-interested corporations, and an international environment preoccupied with responding to evil seems insufficient even on its own terms. Hart wants to combine goodness with greatness, but if a choice has to be made, the message of his book clearly suggests that goodness matters more.

૮૨— As the late historian Christopher Lasch reminds us, there was another tradition of virtue in the United States besides the republican one; inspired more by religion and its preoccupation with sin than by cities and their distrust of plain folk, its greatest theorists were Calvinist theologians such as Jonathan Edwards and his followers. Lasch's magnum opus, *The True and Only Heaven*, which pays considerable attention to this alternative tradition, is a seminal work in the liberal retreat from greatness. "In the late sixties and early seventies," Lasch writes, "Marxism seemed indispensable to me—with the many refinements and modifications introduced by those who rejected the positivistic, mechanistic side of Marxism."[20] Like so many others of his generation, Lasch would turn away from the left. But unlike so many others, he did not transform himself into an anti-Marxist. Instead, Lasch questioned the assumption of progress that linked together, whatever their other differences, Marxism, liberalism, and conservatism.

Lasch's heroes were an odd collection of thinkers, from Ralph Waldo Emerson to Henry George to William James and Josiah Royce. Uniting them was their recognition of the limits nature, God, or man's own fallibility placed on human achievement. Steeped in the values of the lower middle-class, Lasch admired those who defended loyalty over mobility or neighborhood over nation. Lasch was not thoroughly disillusioned; he tried to make a distinction between optimism, which was naive and unrealistic, and hope, which, properly tempered, could produce realistic expectations about what the future might bring. (In similar fashion, he warned against a nostalgic sensibility that, in his view, was simply the flip side of the belief in progress.) But there is no doubting the elegiac tone that pervaded Lasch's work. The enthusiasms and ambitions of the 1960s had crossed an important line, in Lasch's view, threatening such fragile institutions as the family, the church, and the university. It was time to turn down the volume in the hope of salvaging at least something from the cultural upheavals of the period.

In one of his many fascinating asides, Lasch took aim at writers such as Arthur Schlesinger, Jr., Reinhold Niebuhr, and John Kenneth Galbraith who tried to develop a realistic liberalism during the 1950s. (A great admirer of Niebuhr, Lasch wrote that the theologian at one point had forgotten his own warnings about the temptations of power.)[21] The inclusion of Galbraith may come as a surprise to contemporary readers, for Galbraith's 1958 bestseller *The Affluent Society,* a widely read critique of the consumer society emerging in postwar America, could be read as a Puritan-like attack on the dangers of luxury.[22] But as Lasch rightly notes, Galbraith had previously written *American Capitalism: The Concept of Countervailing Power,* which argued that bigness—in government, industry, and labor—was here to stay.[23] Galbraith's message to the left in that book was to stop longing for a society of small producers and to seek instead to check the power of business by strengthening other big institutions.

Galbraith himself would eventually bestow his seal of approval on writers who owed far more to Christopher Lasch than to his own *American Capitalism.* By the 1980s and 1990s, a vision of the good society had begun to emerge on the left that was even more indebted to Puritanism than *The Affluent Society.* Liberals in the immediate postwar period had made their peace with progress in the expectation that economic growth would do more to benefit workers than redistribution. But this seemed an insufficient response to a new generation of more radical critics who began to focus on the downside of capitalism's ever-demanding quest for productivity. Americans, economist Juliet Schor wrote in 1991, were too overworked; productivity had brought with it the potential for people to spend more time with their children and to lead lives of greater leisure, but instead Americans were working harder in every aspect of their lives. They spent their extra hours in overtime instead of enjoying vacations. Household work expanded even as labor-saving promises were offered. And all the extra work brought very little extra happiness, because people tended to spend more with what they earned, thus fueling their need to earn even more to spend.[24]

Not only do we overwork, in other words, we also overspend, the subject of Schor's next book, which appeared in 1998. Here the critique cut deeper, for Schor was not just indicting capitalists for their insidious machinations, but pointing the finger of blame at Americans themselves, who were hardly being forced against their will to buy gas-guzzling cars or second homes. Schor was nonetheless heartened that some chose to resist the pressures to keep up with the Joneses by voluntarily "downshifting" to spend more times with themselves and their families. True, this was hardly the response to capitalist excess associated with the socialist and progressive movements of the past; downshifting, as Schor noted, had more in common with "Quakers, Shakers, transcendentalists, and hippies." But Schor nonetheless praised those who questioned their commitments to work and consumption, for "downshifting often involves soul-searching and a coming to consciousness about a life that may well have been on automatic pilot."[25]

Whether intended or not, Schor's reversion to the language of religion suggests the Calvinist affinities in her work and in turn reveals her debt to Christopher Lasch. The debt is only a partial one; Lasch's sympathies were with lower-middle-class people who had learned to accept their fate, while Schor appealed to upper-middle-class professionals whose commitment to the simple life was more a choice than a command. Still, as Lasch's book among others helps us recognize, the appeal of the simple life has been a constant theme throughout American history and culture, and, as the example of the transcendentalists suggests, has typically been accompanied by spiritual longings.[26] Schor's reservations about progress, her taste for asceticism, and her insistence that strong-willed people can resist the temptations to work too hard and spend too much amount to a secular telling of the Puritan story of the fall from grace. Although she does not use the term, Schor's is a politics of American goodness, very much in line with those thinkers identified by Michael Sandel who put questions of right ahead of considerations of efficiency or size.

Like the religious believer who seeks purity of heart through a born-again experience with Jesus, the quest for the simple life involves individual transformation far more than social regeneration. One does not therefore find in Schor's work, or in other accounts of a leftist politics of consumption, much of a program for social change; Schor's suggestions involve urging people to take CDs out of the local library instead of buying them, and to purchase fewer gifts during holiday periods.[27] Asking Americans whether they shop too much is not quite the same thing as tackling age-old issues of economic inequality or worker participation in industry, as some of Schor's critics on the left have pointed out.[28] Still, Schor's books do seem appropriate to the zeitgeist in which notions of greatness have receded from the left's agenda.

Great critics require great societies and vice versa; it makes sense that a president who aspired to greatness, such as Theodore Roosevelt, would become so annoyed with the muckrakers, for Lincoln Steffans and his colleagues were to social criticism what Roosevelt was to presidential leadership: outsized, ambitious, combative. A leftist politics of consumption, by contrast, seemed perfectly at home in the age of Bill Clinton, focused, as it was, on small things that can be corrected by individual decisions. The appeal of big themes on the left is not over; Barbara Ehenreich's *Nickel and Dimed*, with its implicit homage to George Orwell's

Down and Out in Paris and London, suggests that a more traditional kind of leftist criticism is not only possible, but attractive
enough to reach the best-seller lists.[29] But Ehrenreich's work also
stands out as the exception to a trend that focuses so much on
everyday life that it skips over larger questions of social justice.
The question is whether the left stands for ensuring that those
who get very little from their society can get more or whether
those who get more from their society ought to accept less. Once,
the left's answer would have been unambiguously the former.
Nowadays, it would seem, opinion is split.

⌒— Whether in its Jeffersonian or Calvinist version, republicanism, like anti-Federalism, distrusted anything too large. Such
distrust extended to, and was often principally concerned with,
territory. "At the center of the theoretical expression of Anti-Federalist opposition to increased centralization of power in the national government," Cecelia Kenyon wrote, "was the belief that
republican government was possible only for a relatively small
territory and a relatively small and homogeneous population."[30]
Large government would not only be likely to assemble more
power, all the better to oppress those who stood in its way, it
would also be more open to forms of corruption that would undermine goodness. If anti-Federalists and republicans had lived at
a time when bumper stickers mattered, no doubt they would have
settled on the one that says "small is beautiful."

That expression, of course, was a book before it was a bumper
sticker. Published in 1973 by the British economist E. F. Schumacher, *Small Is Beautiful* was an immediate sensation.[31] Although
the book itself was wordy and often unpersuasive, the title was
brilliantly chosen. In three words, Schumacher captured the spirit
of his age. He understood that for the kinds of well-meaning liber-

als who would be likely to turn to his analysis, bigness had become bad. And nowhere was that more true than in the arena with which Schumacher was most concerned: the way human beings interact with the natural environment.

Preoccupations with the environment are anything but a recent phenomenon in American political thought. So much have attitudes toward nature been intertwined with the meaning of America that we have had not one strain of environmentalist thinking but at least two. Henry David Thoreau was an early exponent of one of them, a tradition that also includes naturalists like John Muir and contemporary advocates of deep ecology. This strain, which is often called pastoral, sees nature as pure and defenseless and in need of considerable protection against human onslaught. The pastoral tradition can take many forms, from those who worry about population growth or resource depletion to those who find in nature an alternative to civilization's artificiality. What characterizes them all is the sense that ecology, and not economics, is the true dismal science. Pastoralists, in the spirit of Christopher Lasch, can never celebrate something called "progress." For them the earth's ability to replenish itself is problematic. Pessimistic toward the future, suspicious of human intention, protective by instinct, the pastoral tradition in ecology shares considerable intellectual turf with the anti-Federalist tradition in politics, which also looked with a wary eye at anyone proclaiming that big might be better. Environmentalism is a global movement, but it finds a specific resonance in an American intellectual tradition that contrasts the natural innocence and purity of this side of the Atlantic with the corruption and decadence of the other.

The other environmental tradition, aptly labeled progressive, dates back to Gifford Pinchot, the first head of America's Forest Service and a Bull Moose activist. The progressive environmentalist does not view nature and civilization as inherently antagonistic;

each can improve the other so long as the right tools can be found for maximizing their potential utility. Management of resources is crucial for progressives, and this emphasis on problem solving leaves little place for a neo-Malthusian pessimism that would distract from the immediate tasks at hand. Nor do progressives share the romantic naturalism of a Thoreau and his twentieth-century epigones; on the contrary, progressives view themselves as hard-nosed realists, willing to consider the trade-off involved when society has to make difficult choices between equally compelling objectives. The language of progressivism is one of trusteeship and stewardship; the land was not put there just to sit there unused or to be treated as an object of spiritual worship but has been placed under collective authority for the benefit of everyone.

As the political scientist Bob Pepperman Taylor argues, these two approaches, which hold to very different conceptions of the nature of nature, also can be contrasted according to their differing conceptions of politics. The pastoral tradition is contemptuous of power and politics and dismissive of the do-good intentions of reformers. Religion, especially prophetic religion, serves as the model for the pastoral style; its basic text is the jeremiad, and its basic stance is uncompromising. Progressives, by contrast, administrative, utilitarian, and technocratic in outlook, respect power and want to obtain their share of it. Forces that would destroy the environment by using it for exploitative purposes, such as big industrial and mining concerns, in their view, are already well organized and motivated, and the only hope to curtail their influence is by organizing a force against them, inevitably using government for that purpose. The prophetic style of protest is not part of their arsenal; labeling the ecological extremists of his day with a word of his own choosing, Pinchot wrote that "I could not join the denudatics, because they were marching up a blind alley. . . . The job was not to stop the ax, but to regulate its use."[32]

Because they differ so much in their underlying assumptions about politics, the pastoral and progressive traditions in environmental thought have sharply contrasting perspectives on the question of American greatness. When he called himself a "true patriot," Thoreau was not dissembling; his writings are filled with love of his country, especially as it contrasts with Europe. "If the heavens of America appear infinitely higher, and the stars brighter, I trust that these facts are symbolical of the height to which the philosophy and poetry and religion of her inhabitants may one day soar," he wrote in "Walking." But the greatness to which America aspired did not, and could not, originate in Washington. In "Civil Disobedience," Thoreau had much to say about one of the figures who stands tall in any treatment of American greatness: Daniel Webster. Thoreau liked him. "Compared with the cheap professions of most reformers, and the still cheaper wisdom and eloquence of politicians in general," he wrote, "his are almost the only sensible and valuable words." But Webster's quest for a great country was, in Thoreau's opinion, a futile one because it put its faith in civilized, and therefore transient, things and, in any case, Thoreau lost his appreciation for Webster after the latter supported the Compromise of 1850. Politics was simply not in Thoreau's blood. "Hope and the future for me are not in lawns and cultivated fields, not in towns and cities, but in the impervious and quaking swamps."[33]

Pinchot, by comparison, was not only a political activist closely identified with American greatness advocate Theodore Roosevelt, he also linked his concern with land management to the future strength of his country. "The conservation of natural resources is the basis, and the only permanent basis, of national success," he wrote. For Pinchot, natural resources were not sacred and otherworldly but an indispensable ingredient for human happiness; in his exuberantly optimistic outlook on the world, scientific management applied to the land as a precondition of democratic equality. As he put the matter in his manifesto: "I stand for the Roosevelt policies because they set the common good of all of us above the private gain of some of us; because they recognize the livelihood of the small man as more important to the Nation than the profit of the big man." Pinchot's vision may well have been too optimistic; corporate interests would prove to have little trouble dominating the agencies established by Progressives to regulate them. But there is no doubting that for him, "the great fundamental problem" is one with which Hamilton and Marshall would feel a sense of kinship: "shall we continue, as a Nation, to exist in well-being?" Nor can we doubt that his answer is that we could, so long as we applied principles of rational planning and allocation as much to the natural world as to the industrial.[34]

Although Pinchot must surely have thought that his approach to the environment, tied as it was to modern techniques of scientific management, would be the one that would prevail, the pastoral tradition is the more influential among contemporary writers concerned with the environment. Like Thoreau, Wendell Berry is an American patriot; a recent collection of his essays is dedicated to the signers of the Declaration of Independence. This may explain why the America he evokes has such an eighteenth-century feel about it; the independence he desires his nation to have "can be maintained only [by] the most practical economic self-reliance. At the very least, a nation should be able sustainably to feed, clothe, and shelter its citizens, using its own sources and by its own work." Many of the Declaration's signatories, moreover, considered themselves citizens of their states, as does Berry, who has strong loyalties to Kentucky and the South of which it is a part; he admires the Southern manifesto *I'll Take My Stand* for "its astute and uncompromising regionalism" and finds himself relatively untroubled by its segregationist origins. Berry's agragrarianism fits into no existing political camp, which is clearly how he likes it. Distrustful of movements, even those dear to his own heart, he writes, not to shape elections and policies, but as an elegiac essayist and poet.[35]

Bill McKibben also writes in the shadow of Thoreau, even if he finds Thoreau "intensely anthropocentric." We should not make Thoreau's mistake of valuing nature because nature is valuable to human beings, McKibben insists; instead we need what he calls a "humble philosophy" that appreciates that "the rest of creation mattered for its own sake, and that man didn't matter all that much."[36] Progressive environmentalists want to conserve nature to further human happiness, but human happiness is just not all that important to McKibben: who are we, he frequently asks, to think that nature owes us anything? In his more recent work, McKibben extends the same reasoning to contemporary genetic engineering and research into robotics and artificial intelligence. There should be something called an "enough point," he argues, that would enable us to draw a line in the sand and to say that beyond this, we will not go. McKibben himself will not go so far as therapeutic cloning, for if we allowed that, he believes, we would be unable to stop the rush toward human cloning. And to the point that his concerns might make him seem an ally of the Christian right, McKibben responds, correctly, that a number of people on the left—Judy Norsigian, one of the feminist authors of *Our Bodies, Ourselves* and former New Leftists Tom Hayden and Todd Gitlin—have expressed similar reservations.[37] While there certainly are compelling moral reasons to raise alarms about the prospect of human cloning—therapeutic cloning is another matter entirely—there also can be found on the left a fear that in the face of the unknown gains and losses associated with scientific advances, the most prudential course is one of wariness rather than enthusiasm.

The pastoral tradition may have strong appeal among writers with a prophetic sensibility, but we would expect, given its antipolitical character, that it would have little attraction to politicians, who, as seekers after power, ought to be more sympathetic to the progressive inclination. This is not, in fact, how matters have worked themselves out. As Taylor correctly observes, the contemporary political figure who comes closest to embodying Pinchot's progressive scientific management is actually one of the more forgotten recent minority-party candidates for president, Barry Commoner.[38] Commoner, unlike Pinchot, was a socialist, yet like the earlier man, both his science and his politics were devoted to securing natural resources for improved human use and to furthering the quest for social justice. Commoner rejected neo-Malthusian formulations of the environmental problem and their dour pessimism, barely concealed misanthropy, and attacks on economic growth in any form. Be more willing to confront private industry than Pinchot was, Commoner argued, and you could begin to make progress on the environmental front.

By contrast, pastoral visions of the environment have featured prominently in the thoughts of a number of prominent officeholders, including William O. Douglas, Stewart Udall, and, not surprising given his taste for eighteenth-century republican virtue, Gary Hart. In more recent times, the pastoral tradition has, if anything, increased its saliency for liberal politicians; in sharp contrast to Commoner's relative obscurity, two of the candidates in the 2000 election were closer to the pastoral tradition than the progressive one. One of them, Ralph Nader, has been both a critic of corporate capitalism—he is, for example, very much in the anti-spending camp of Juliet Schor[39]—and an advocate for the environment, and, despite his running, at least the first time around, on the Green Party ticket, Nader's recent speeches and activities have concentrated more on his economic populism than his ecological awareness. Still, Nader shares much in common with the Thoreauvian strain in American political thought.

Ralph Nader grew up fascinated by "outsiders," as he called them, prophets such as John Muir, Ida Tarbell, and Jeanette Rankin who were willing to denounce the machinations of Washington insiders. Nader believes in what he calls "authentic" democracy, in which, as in the classic film *Mr. Smith Goes to Washington*, the voices of ordinary people drive the corrupt from the halls of power.[40] Such a vision of politics has its roots in both the progressive as well as the pastoral tradition in environmental thought, but if there are any doubts that Nader belongs primarily in the American goodness camp, he dispelled them when he chose to run for president in 2000 and then, remarkably, chose to run again in 2004, even though his argument that the two parties are indistinguishable had lost so much credibility that even he had abandoned it. Third-party candidates are spoilers, and what they try to spoil is the possibility of majority government. While Nader fills his speeches and writings with appeals to social justice, there is little doubt that his commitments to purifying what he views as an evil system of politics takes priority over his outrage at the unjust policies of either of the two dominant parties. Like so many adherents before him to a politics of goodness, Ralph Nader prefers abstractions and principles to real-life dilemmas, as if the only point of politics is to make a point. A world in which the evils he identifies are reduced because leaders are willing to make pragmatic compromises for the sake of social improvement is a world of little interest to him.

The other candidate in the 2000 campaign with an interest in ecology was, of course, Al Gore. *Earth in the Balance*, his ecological manifesto, was, as Republicans were quick to point out, a most unusual book for a major party presidential candidate to have written. The book does not lack for ambition; Gore calls for an international campaign rivaling the Marshall Plan to address the environmental crisis. Yet what is most striking about Gore's approach is its relentless pessimism. The environmental crisis, he writes, "serves as a kind of mirror in which we are able to see ourselves more clearly if we are willing to question more deeply who we are and who we want to be, both as individuals and as a civilization." Neither the people nor the society held up to that mirror have flattering images. Turning to some of the most depressing modern authors one can find—among them R. D. Laing, Gregory Bateson, and Alice Miller—Gore compares contemporary civilization to a dysfunctional family committed to endless cycles of addiction. No addiction is more powerful, in Gore's view, than the one "to the consumption of the earth itself. This addictive relationship distracts us from the pain of what we have lost: a direct experience of our connection to the vividness, vibrancy, and aliveness of the rest of the natural world."[41]

Concerned so much with climate, waste, food, forests, and oceans, *Earth in the Balance* has relatively little to say about human beings. The book therefore shares more with Bill McKibben's hostility toward progress than it does with Gifford Pinchot's sense that progress can serve the cause of human equality. Indeed, social justice never registers as a theme in *Earth in the Balance*, as if matters so this-worldly as taxation or the welfare state should not interrupt deep thinking about Heideggarian preoccupations with the nature of Being. Gore does deal with one earthly matter that has allowed the less well off to participate in some of life's satisfactions: consumption. But, as one might expect, he treats the phenomenon, not unlike Juliet Schor, with heavy-handed disdain. *Earth in the Balance* strives for spiritual truth, not political reform. At least thinkers like Lani Guinier who reach back to the eighteenth-century are still within the purview of the Enlightenment; Albert Gore harks back to a period long before that when people, or so we are expected to believe, lived in a more organic relationship with the natural world around them.

The claims Gore makes in his book, like those of Berry and McKibben, rest at some level on scientific evidence that politicians and polemicists are not well equipped to address. (I count myself among those so ill equipped.) If indeed energy resources are soon to be depleted, food supplies to be exhausted, and global warming about to unleash flooding not seen since Noah, all earthly matters, including the question of whether one particular country can ever again reclaim its greatness, do come to seem trivial. Alas for the cause of certainty, the scientific data are far from definitive; skeptical accounts of the earth's environmental crisis have appeared, and at least some predictions of doom, including those of progressive environmentalists such as Barry Commoner, have not yet born fruit.[42] But even if claims of a crisis serious enough to warrant immediate attention are granted, the question is still open about the most effective way to respond. Because that question is political rather than scientific, it is worth pondering why a politician of the stature of Al Gore would reach, as if instinctively, for a tradition that has historically rejected politics, skipping almost entirely over another one that tied the question of environmental preservation to questions of American power and success.

The answer, I believe, lies in the turn against progress that has led so many on the left to take a second look at the anti-Federalists and the tradition of civic republicanism. At least since the time of Edmund Burke, conservatives have questioned the notion that bigger and newer implies better, but that essentially reactive temperament now seems to characterize the way the American left approaches nearly all the issues it confronts; one could not imagine a Republican conservative writing a book as filled with doomsday scenarios as Al Gore's. Fear of the future has seemingly shifted from one political party to the other; Democrats today are as unlikely to call for Kennedy-like ventures into space—George W. Bush has in any case preempted them on that front, even if his fiscal policy, allowing no room to finance any such activities, led him to drop the idea within weeks after it was proposed—as they are to manifest Pinchot-like confidence in government. In this mood of retreat from big government and economic growth, environmentalism, especially in its antipolitical form, seems the inevitable outcome. If small is beautiful, American greatness, a big project if there ever was one, must be especially ugly.

✑— From the perspective of American greatness, the slogan of the environmental movement—"think globally, act locally"—is particularly revealing. For the one thing that the global and the local have in common is that neither represents the national. With our thoughts directed to the rest of the world, indeed to the universe of which it is a part, while our actions are confined to families and friends at home, we never have to think about the political community in between, the one that requires as much care and cultivation as the natural environment to flourish and survive. Suspect on the left for its complicity with imperialism since at least the time of the Vietnam War, the American nation is now viewed by a significant number of left-leaning intellectuals as a hegemonic force whose expansionist tendencies must be resisted.

Death of a Nation is the title given to a book by David W. Noble, and the title was not meant as a lament.[43] In the view of Noble, "the nation" is a value-laden term, an ideological construct designed to make Americans believe that their society is different from and better than any other society. Noble equates the nation with efforts capitalist elites have made to impose their imperialistic designs on the rest of the world, as well as by efforts by white Anglo-Saxon Protestants to impose their values on Americans at home who are different from them. In choosing his title, Noble did not mean to imply that the American nation had lost its power; on the contrary, its tentacles, he believes, reach everywhere. But knowing what we now know about America's awful racism at home and global designs abroad, scholars such as Noble have begun to treat the nation as if it should indeed rest in peace.

Noble, writes George Lipsitz in his introduction to *Death of a Nation*, is "one of the few people in his generational cohort to remain intellectually and politically alert to the new possibilities emerging from contemporary contradictions and conflicts."[44] In that he is correct; Noble's attack on the idea of the American nation resonates strongly with contemporary scholars in the discipline of American studies, who have turned their professional association and scholarly activities into an attack on the United States striking in its vehemence.[45] The founders of the discipline of American studies—Perry Miller, Vernon K. Parrington, Henry Nash Smith, Leo Marx—were, academically speaking, the progressives of their day, similar in their outlook to James MacGregor Burns and Cecelia Kenyon. Not only did they attempt to provide a coherent narrative about how an American nation came into being, there was, in their work, a sense of discovery; they found greatness in a literature—Hawthorne, Twain, Fitzgerald—typically dismissed by the guardians of high culture with their eyes on Great Britain. The American studies of earlier generations did not ignore social problems—class stratification featured in their work, and Marx's *The Machine in the Garden* would anticipate environmental preoccupations—but it was also an optimistic field because the America it studied was an optimistic society. To be sure there was an emphasis on consensus, and a resulting avoidance of conflict, in much of this literature. But that, too, was progressive for its time; by developing a national narrative, early exemplars of American studies were extending the concern of nineteenth-century political reformers to fashion a society in which everyone had a place.

Contemporary students of American studies, by contrast, want, as one of the leading scholars in the field, Jan Radway, puts it, "to complicate and fracture the very idea of an American nation."[46] For Radway and her colleagues, the term "America" is on the one hand an imperialist pretension—there are other nations that have a claim to the name, writers in his camp are fond of noting—and on the other an empty shell, signifying, as it does, a futile effort to put boundaries of space and time around a fluid global reality. Creating and sustaining the American nation is as dangerous to the world as fashioning a coherent political majority, spending on consumer goods, or using the environment to advance human purpose. Nations, especially the American nation, are big things; fracturing them is a way of trying to make them smaller.

One of the more interesting aspects of this attack from the left on the idea of the nation is how smoothly it intersects with a similar attack from the right not that long ago. From Lincoln through the two Roosevelts and into the era of Kennedy and Johnson, the idea of the nation has traditionally been resisted by the right and embraced by those who believed in such progressive ideas as equality. Nowadays, the roles have been reversed.

It is impossible to exaggerate the fear and loathing of the nation expressed by conservatives throughout American history. "There is," as Kentucky Senator James B. Beck expressed the thought in 1875, "that contemptible word *Nation*—a word which no good Democrat uses, when he can find any other, and when forced to use it, utters in disgust."[47] For men such as Beck, the idea of the nation implied equality for all those guaranteed citizenship within it; standing firm against the principle of nationhood was a price worth paying to keep the races apart. In the years after Beck expressed his views, moreover, conservatives kept up the attack; Southerners like M. E. Bradford, although he was a Republican rather than a Democrat, were as hostile to the nation as James Beck. When economics equaled race as the major issue in the South, conservatives were offered an additional reason to oppose the principle of American nationality, for as the national government came to be relied upon to regulate the extremes of the market, protecting private interest required attacking national power. Conservatives, in other words, have been second to none in their assertions of patriotism, but they have also been typically last in their commitment to nationalism.

For those speaking in defense of equality, on the other hand, the nation came to be viewed as an indispensable ally. "When a group of abolitionists established a postwar magazine designed to carry on in the spirit of Garrison's *Liberator*," historian Morton Keller points out, "*The Nation* seemed an eminently appropriate name."[48] (One wonders whether the editors of the same magazine today, firmly committed to frequent attacks on American power, ponder changing its name.) Former abolitionists, of course, generally believed that the most pressing form of inequality was the one between the races that seemed so curiously persistent even after so much blood had been shed to bring about its eventual elimination. But the same linkage between equality and the idea of the nation could be extended to arenas other than race. Theodore Roosevelt's "New Nationalism" illustrates one such linkage. "As a New Yorker," historian Gary Gerstle writes of TR, "he understood how large a proportion of the working class comprised immigrants and their children. His New Nationalist program was meant to bring them into the nation, not just politically and culturally, but economically as well."[49] As Roosevelt's life and career demonstrated, nationalism could indeed have its racist and imperialist sides, yet without it, citizenship for all was an impossibility.

This history ought to give contemporary scholars of American studies pause when they contemplate fracturing the nation they are trying to study. There is no doubt of their hostility toward the idea; in an especially unpleasant episode, the literary theorist Barbara Hernnstein Smith responded to E. D. Hirsch's suggestion that students might be made more aware of the history and culture of their nation with over-the-top sarcasm: "Wild applause; fireworks; music—*America the Beautiful*; all together, now: *Calvin Coolidge, Gunga Din, Peter Pan, spontaneous combustion.* Hurrah for America and the national culture! Hurrah!"[50] Leftist intellectuals, it would seem, can be as contemptuous of the idea of the nation as Kentucky's Senator Beck was in 1875. Properly speaking, these intellectuals cannot be identified as adherents to the camp of American goodness; they are the kind of thinkers who would attack a term like "good" as hopelessly impossible to define with precision and as dangerous if it somehow could be. But even though they lack a vision of what America should stand for—it is one thing to argue that the nation stands for the wrong things and another thing entirely to argue that there is not, nor should there by, any such thing as the nation at all—they have taken the fear of American greatness characteristic of the American left to its extreme position. So long as politics remains the only method of achieving common objectives, and so long as politics takes place within nation-states, calling for the death of the American nation is an effective formula for irrelevance, perhaps a fortunate outcome when those of this persuasion have so little to offer positively in the first place.

⌒— "Do we really want an America of 500 million people?" This was only one of the difficult questions asked by former Colorado governor Richard Lamm in 1995. "How big a country do we want to become? What problem in America will be made better by continuing to add massive numbers of people? . . . Immigration will decide whether we stabilize or whether we continue to grow."[51] Lamm, once widely respected for his environmentalist sympathies, has, in his subsequent career as a doomsday prophet, displayed a knack for controversy. Concerned that the number of people living in the United States is exceeding the capacity of America's environment to sustain them, he gained national notoriety for his suggestion that the elderly have "a duty to die."[52] He aroused the ire of the Christian right for his unabashed defense of abortion. And, as his 1995 comment suggested, he had no qualms in attacking the immigration reforms of the 1960s in the name of ecological sustainability.

Immigration is a test case of attitudes toward American greatness. Great societies, especially those willing and anxious to play a role in world affairs, require large populations, and particularly at a time of declining birthrates in advanced industrial societies, one of the only ways to expand a country's population is through immigration. There is, in addition, a seemingly inevitable association between immigration and urbanization; while surprisingly large numbers of recent immigrants have moved quickly to suburbs and even to small towns, most remain in cities, revitalizing them with new businesses, ethnic restaurants, and multilingual complexity—and in so doing, placed themselves in opposition to visions of American pastoralism. The presence of large numbers of immigrants ensures that a society will be actively involved in global politics, as immigrants and their children frequently demand that the United States take an interest in what is happening back in Poland or Mexico. For all these reasons, pro-immigration sentiment will typically be associated with the idea that the United States ought to be a cosmopolitan society willing to expand at home and abroad, while ideas hostile to immigration will resonate more with traditions emphasizing republican virtue—an idea, after all, associated with the Protestant origins of the United States—and limited government.

One example of this relationship between American greatness and sympathy toward immigration can be cited from the same period in which James MacGregor Burns and Cecelia Kenyon wrote their analyses on the insufficiencies of America's eighteenth-century political origins. John F. Kennedy, then a senator from Massachusetts, published *A Nation of Immigrants* in 1958, in which he urged an end to America's system of national quotas, a shortsighted policy that, in Kennedy's view, gave insufficient appreciation to meritocratic principles in favor of distinctions that smacked of racism. Kennedy was revising his book at the time of his death, and in a posthumously published edition, his brother Robert cited it in support of what would eventually become the immigration reforms of 1965.[53] There were obvious partisan reasons for Kennedy's stance; immigrants and their children typically voted Democratic. At the same time, one reason they did so was that Democrats, at least the Northern branch to which Kennedy belonged, welcomed them and, in so doing, stood for a more capacious understanding of what America ought to be.

As if little has changed since Kennedy wrote his book, opposition to immigration, along today's ideological spectrum, is more likely to be found on the right than on the left. Former California governor Pete Wilson was the first prominent contemporary politician to appeal overtly to anti-immigrant sentiment in recent years, and even though the Republican Party has all but repudiated his position in search of Hispanic votes, the attempt by President Bush to allow some illegal aliens to gain legal status aroused considerable hostility from conservative Republicans in Congress. The most extreme anti-immigrant politician in America, Patrick Buchanan, his recent populism notwithstanding, is among the most conservative.

And in 2004 the American debate over immigration intensified when one of the most brilliant of American conservative thinkers, Samuel P. Huntington, joined it with the publication of his book *Who Are We?*, his passionate, and proudly nativist, attack on immigrants in general and Mexican immigrants in particular.[54]

Despite the fact that Republicans and conservatives are more likely to support immigration restriction than liberals, however, it would be a mistake to conclude that attitudes toward immigration line up according to the prevailing political ideologies. This has certainly never been true historically in America. Booker T. Washington's call for restrictions on foreign labor in his 1895 Atlanta Exposition address is a relatively typical expression of the wariness that African Americans have shown to open borders, no doubt reflecting a not-unjustified fear that low wages offered to immigrants would contribute to black unemployment or underemployment.[55] In similar fashion, the cause of immigration has generally been taken up by business and opposed by labor; the Knights of Labor, an organization cited by Michael Sandel for its openness to republican conceptions of virtue, took the lead in sponsoring the 1885 Contract Labor Act designed to hold down the number of immigrants.[56] Nineteenth-century conservationists such as George Perkins Marshall, "though never a Know-Nothing," as his biographer has written, "shared their qualms about immigration," especially at a time when so many immigrants were Catholic.[57] Birth-control advocate Margaret Sanger, an enthusiast for eugenics, was a firm opponent of immigration, as were many similar protofeminist activists of the 1920s.[58] It was not until the New Deal won the overwhelming support of immigrants and their children that the left could be counted on to celebrate the benefits of a more polyglot America.

Even today there remain legacies of the left's less than enthusiastic welcoming of immigrants. Richard Lamm's concerns about overpopulation reflect the splits that have emerged in environmental groups such as the Sierra Club over the issue. In asking if multiculturalism is bad for women, the late political philosopher Susan Moller Okin raised the question of whether feminists should adopt an attitude prevalent in Europe, which worries that traditionally religious immigrants bring with them attitudes that could setback the struggles for personal liberation that grew out of the 1960s and 1970s.[59] Immigration was not a major issue on the Democratic side in the 2004 campaign, especially because immigrant voters, with significant exceptions among Cubans and some Asians, generally vote Democratic (and because Republicans made a strong play for their votes). Still, there is emerging in the United States a concern with the outsourcing of jobs, and in their efforts to offer American workers at least some protection against globalization, Democratic leaders may find themselves in the near future wondering out loud whether increased immigration can be tolerated at a time when job loss within the traditional Democratic base becomes so pronounced. Should that occur, it is quite conceivable that organized labor, which has softened its opposition to immigration in recent years in favor of organizing immigrants, would return to its traditional hostility toward newcomers.

The one conspicuous example of pro-immigrant sentiment on the left lies in its enthusiasm for multiculturalism. Welcoming immigrants to the United States in the name of diversity therefore offers the left an opportunity to overcome the suspicion toward American greatness associated with its longing for eighteenth-century forms of government. Yet even though America's multicultural left supports immigration, the important question is not how many new arrivals they want to welcome to America but what kind of America they want to welcome them. Two contrasting understandings of the relationship between immigrants and the country to which they move frame the debate over this question. One insists that the primary source of identity, for both immigrants and the society that receives them, is cultural; Americans are likely to insist that immigrants accept aspects of their culture, including English as its language and perhaps even Christianity as its religion, while immigrants, if they are to retain respect for their origins, language, and identity, must respond by keeping aspects of their native culture intact against the majority's demands. The other way of understanding what is at stake when immigrants arrive is creedal; from this point of view, America is not defined by any particular culture but instead by the beliefs to which all are Americans are expected to subscribe, which in turn means that immigrants are obligated to pledge their allegiance to fundamental American ideals, whatever their cultural, religious, or linguistic background.

Before the immigration reforms of 1965, most immigrants, while retaining what sociologist Herbert Gans calls "symbolic" attachments to their ethnicity,[60] were anxious to be accepted and thus willing to shed significant aspects of the culture they brought with them, including, in some cases, their Italian or Jewish names. Whatever loss of identity they may have suffered as a result, their willingness not to insist too strongly on ethnic retainment facilitated the process of adjustment for both them and the country that received them. "Throughout our history," the historian Stephan Thernstrom has written, "the vast majority of immigrants have been absorbed into the nation—and with impressive speed."[61] Will this change now that the bulk of immigrants come from non-European countries? Thernstrom sees no reason to conclude that it will; assimilation, he believes, is not only alive and well, but ought to serve as a warning against classifying Americans by race or country of national origin. Thernstrom is a political conservative, but his position is shared by a number of liberals. We are unlikely to know whether Arthur Schlesinger, Jr., who was a close advisor to John F. Kennedy, did the actual writing of the then senator's 1958 book, but many years later, Schlesinger would publish one of his own, which, while attacking some extreme forms of multiculturalism, restated the case for the assimilation of immigrants, citing, along the way, Stephan Thernstrom in support of his position.[62]

For writers such as Thernstrom and Schlesinger, immigration works best when cultural identities assume less importance than creedal ones. American culture, from this perspective, is not something we inherited from Great Britain and have passed on through the years to everyone else. "The symbols and ceremonies of American citizenship could not be drawn from the political culture or history of British-Americans," Michael Walzer has written. "Our Congress is not a Commons"; Guy Fawkes Day "is not an American holiday; the Magna Carta has never been one of our sacred texts." There being no distinct culture to which immigrants must adopt, we instead seek to emphasize the ideals we share in common, which is why, in Walzer's view, we are united by "symbols and ceremonies [that] are culturally anonymous, invented rather than inherited, voluntaristic in style, narrowly political in context: the flag, the Pledge, the Fourth, the Constitution."[63] What does it mean to be an American? From the standpoint of creed, it means identifying with a political nation, not a cultural one.

A very different sense of the stakes involved in immigration emerges from the writings of those more sympathetic to multiculturalism than Thernstrom and Schlesinger. Although the leading theorists of multiculturalism, such as Will Kymlicka and Charles Taylor, are Canadian, they often uses examples from the United States, and their ideas have had significant appeal among American thinkers. Kymlicka, the more explicitly political of the two, believes that allowing groups to have certain rights—such as those reflected in affirmative action or in programs supporting bilingualism—in no way threatens the individualism upon which liberal democracy is built and may indeed strengthen it by giving the members of minority groups a sense of empowerment and confidence. Not only does multiculturalism serve the interests of justice based on liberal premises, he continues, it is no particular threat to the unity of the social order; whether or not multiculturalism undermines social unity is an empirical, not a theoretical, question, and in his view no evidence has ever been presented demonstrating that it does. There is, therefore, no reason to insist that immigrants abandon the cultures of their origin when they arrive in North America; indeed, justice requires that we allow them to keep as much of their cultural identity as possible. Kymlicka not only disagrees with assimilationists such as Arthur Schlesinger, Jr., he condemns them for their "incomprehensibly paranoid misinterpretations of immigrant multiculturalism."[64]

Just as creedalists come in both conservative (Thernstrom) and liberal (Schlesinger) varieties, so do culturalists. Conservatives, of course, frequently disdain the kinds of multiculturalism that writers like Kymlicka advocate; when not putting the blame for the decline of American ideals on the shoulders of multinational businessmen, for example, Samuel P. Huntington points his finger at the multicultural left, whose cultural relativism and attacks on American history, he believes, have left Americans without an appreciation for the importance of their own traditions. Yet Kymlicka and Huntington have more in common than one might think; Kymlicka, for his part, gives greater priority to minority cultures that already live within a country than to minorities who recently arrive there, which means, in the Canadian context, that he supports the efforts by Quebec to protect the French language even if doing so leads to restrictions on the rights of English-speaking immigrants to Quebec who come from the British Commonwealth. And Huntington, for his part, sounds very much like a leftist when he cites the political scientist Rogers Smith's argument that the ubiquity of the American creed "is at best a half-truth," since, in Huntington's view, "Americans enslaved and then segregated blacks, massacred and marginalized Indians, excluded Asians, discriminated against Catholics, and obstructed immigration by people from outside northwestern Europe."[65]

Huntington and Kymlicka obviously differ over which culture ought to dominate; for the latter, minority cultures, with the exception of Quebec, receive the benefit of the doubt, while for the former, American cultural identity was shaped at the founding by Anglo-Protestantism, and the United States must retain that culture today if it is to remain unified. Understood politically, Huntington and Kymlicka are on different sides. Understood culturally, however, they are on the same side, which may explain why Huntington not only cites Kymlicka favorably in his book, he borrows liberally from nearly all the leftist writers with whose multicultural sympathies he so strongly disagrees. Huntington credits American studies scholar George Lipsitz, of *Death of a Nation* fame, for evidence that American patriotism had begun to fade after the 1960s. Although Benedict Anderson, in his brilliant book *Imagined Communities*, treats nations as actually existing phenomena, expresses admiration for the consistency with which nineteenth- and twentieth-century nationalists rejected appeals to racism, notes that Latin American countries willingly borrowed their republican ideals from the United States, and spends only a handful of pages on North America, both leftist scholars and Huntington rely on his book to suggest that the American nation is an artificially constructed thing, brought together for specific historical purposes that can just as easily be wished out of existence.[66] The black activist Harold Cruse was correct, in Huntington's view, when he wrote that "America is a nation that lies to itself about who and what it is. It is a nation of minorities ruled by a minority of one—it thinks and acts as if it were a nation of white Anglo-Saxon Protestants." Huntington even cites the field of "whiteness studies," perhaps the most radical of all the multiculturalist trends in the humanities, to remind us that all immigrants, including presumably white ones like the Irish, had to adopt Anglo-Protestant culture if they were to succeed in their new land.[67]

However encouraging it may be to witness people of such different views in agreement, the concept around which Huntington and the multiculturalists agree, that of culture, is less helpful to the idea of American greatness than the idea of a creed. Membership in a culture and belief in a creed represent two very different kinds of goods. Cultural identity is ascribed while creedal identity, as Walzer notes, is achieved. Although both culture and creed can change, cultural change takes longer, usually more than one generation, and, at least according to multiculturalists, should be discouraged even when it is possible, whereas creedal identity requires a change of mind rather than a change of body and, at least according to assimilationists, is desirable and ought to be facilitated. Since culture accumulates slowly over time, highlighting it emphasizes the past; since creed holds out aspirations, fidelity to it emphasizes the future. Culture tells us what we cannot do; creed gives us permission to do what once was forbidden. When we listen to our culture, we feel secure and connected. When we respond to our creed, we imagine ourselves free and open to others. A nation built on culture places significant obstacles in its path to greatness. A nation unified by creed challenges itself to live up to its ideals.

The differences between culture and creed lie at the heart of the distinction Michael Igantieff makes between "ethnic" and "civic" nationalism, just as they overlap with David Hollinger's contrast between pluralism and cosmopolitanism. Civic nationalism, as Igantieff uses the term, emphasizes, not race or ethnicity, but the "nation as a community of equal, rights-bearing citizens, united in patriotic attachment to a shared set of political practices and values."[68] Along similar lines, cosmopolitanism, in Hollinger's analysis, unlike pluralism, recognizes difference but allows choice. "A post-ethnic perspective denies neither history nor biology, nor the need for affiliations, but it does deny that history and biology provide a set of clear orders for the affiliations we are to make."[69] Both of these writers understand that there is a link between immigration, diversity, and American greatness, *and* that such a link must necessarily reject the notion that culture is destiny. Culture is too immutable a phenomenon to allow for the dynamism and growth that a mature and ambitious polity requires.

So long as they assign culture the priority they do, neither strong defenders of multiculturalism nor advocates for American cultural hegemony can make an argument on behalf of societal greatness. Ambition, unity within diversity, and cosmopolitanism are as suspect in the one as they are in the other. Both trends in contemporary American thought seem to recognize this. The academic left attacks the nation-state for being insufficiently cosmopolitan from the perspective of globalism, but just when one might think that its horizons are being lifted, it turns around and lowers them by defending ethnic parochialism against the cosmopolitanism of the nation-state. The same course is taken in reverse by conservative culturalists; Huntington, for example, long known as a realist defender of an American leadership in pursuit of greatness, transforms himself into something of a romantic populist, in making his case against immigration. To limit Americans in terms of their numbers or identities is to limit America in its aspirations.

It is to the credit of the left that it has risen to the defense of diversity in the face of cultural nationalism. It is a shame that it has done so in terms of identities that remain frozen. Hollinger's distinction between identity and affiliation is important here; a politics based on the former is involuntary and touched with coercion—our identities are chosen for us—while one based on the affiliations we choose is inherently more liberal and open. American greatness in the present and future can best be served as it was in the past: by opening up borders to admit large numbers of potential new citizens, and then by insisting on the centrality of national citizenship in shaping the identity of those who arrive here.

᠙— Something happened to the Democratic Party as its leaders during the 1960s, John F. Kennedy and Lyndon Johnson, found themselves embroiled in Vietnam. Although Democrats had achieved power in postwar America by emphasizing their commitment to a strong national defense, the Cold War consensus within the party was frail; some on the left, admirers of one sort or another of the Soviet Union, distrusted the Cold War from the start, and others began to question nuclear brinkmanship as it was operationalized during the Kennedy administration. In any case, Vietnam split the party in two, sending the hawks in the direction of neoconservatism and Republicanism while convincing the doves that ambitious foreign policy undertakings ought to be avoided at all cost. Although historically it had been Republicans and conservatives who were America's true isolationists, by the time Jimmy Carter and Bill Clinton managed to get themselves elected president, the tendency to withdraw from the world's problems had shifted parties and ideological coloration.

Domestic and foreign ambitions, as much as liberals these days like to separate them, are inevitably linked; the more the Democratic Party viewed itself as fighting the Cold War, the stronger was its commitment to domestic reform, and, conversely, the turn against international intervention abroad seemed to match the mood of resignation so prevalent at home. As it did, the "Vietnam syndrome"—the foreign policy paralysis that took over the Democratic Party, and to some degree the nation as well, in the wake of the inability of the United States to win the war—reinforced all the themes that had led the American left in the course of the previous fifty years to question its once-strong sympathies toward centralized government, economic growth, environmental management, the idea of the nation, and increased immigration. The greater the Vietnam War grew in intensity, the further back in history liberals looked to oppose it. Prominent critics of the war, such as Arkansas senator J. William Fulbright, held positions on domestic issues that were more reminiscent of John C. Calhoun than they were of John Marshall (a pattern that would be repeated when another Southern senator not known as a friend of racial equality, Robert Byrd of West Virginia, took the lead in opposing the war in Iraq). Many more to the left than Fulbright went even further back; speaking at a 1965 rally against the war, the then president of Students for a Democratic Society, Carl Oglesby, described Thomas Jefferson and Thomas Paine as "heroes" and wondered what they would have to say to Lyndon Johnson and McGeorge Bundy.[70] The eighteenth century hovered over the spirit of the antiwar movement; historian Howard Zinn, for example, described the North Vietnamese as eighteenth-century Jeffersonians committed to our Declaration of Independence, not as twentieth-century communists with a soft spot for Josef Stalin.[71]

By looking so longingly on a time when goodness so clearly triumphed over greatness, opponents of the War in Vietnam began to question nearly all of their assumptions about the need for centralized power to achieve liberal objectives. Even a far more moderate voice than Zinn's, Arthur Schlesinger, Jr., a strong advocate for liberal ambition in the 1950s and 1960s, wrote about an "imperial presidency" in ways that, in its invocation of the Founders and their commitments to the separation of powers, seemed to have more in common with Lani Guinier's later fears than it did with the earlier hopes of James MacGregor Burns.[72] In this sense, the Vietnam Syndrome long outlasted the Vietnam War. No one should doubt that the rise of conservatism since the 1980s is primarily attributable to the political skills and determination of conservative activists.[73] But nor can it be denied that the right flourished because the left, having begun to question ambition in Southeast Asia, began to lose its taste for great ventures in all spheres of political life.

September 11 might have led to a change of heart among many on the left, but it was followed so quickly by the War in Iraq, and the War in Iraq, in turn transformed itself with such speed into a quagmire resembling Vietnam, that leftist critics took up in opposing this war where they left off in opposing the earlier one. Once again, the eighteenth century, with its implication of unspoiled goodness, became the alternative against which to compare the imperialistic pretensions of the Bush foreign policy makers. "All those who really love this country are obliged to resurrect the legacy of Jefferson and Madison, so that the anti-democratic legacy does not prevail," wrote media critic Mark Crispin Miller.[74] For T. D. Allman, another critic of the Bush policies, Jefferson and the Founding Fathers adhered to the twin principles of separation of powers at home and noninvolvement abroad because they "did not pretend that Americans were somehow exempt from the temptations that corrupt people of other nationalities."[75] War in Iraq undermined both principles; not only did we search for devils overseas, which John Quincy Adams warned us not to do, but we put all the power in the hands of one man in order to do so. Thomas Paine "wouldn't have had much trouble recognizing the Bush administration as Federalist in sentiment, 'monarchical' and 'aristocratical' in its actions, royalist in its mistrust of freedom, imperialist in the bluster of its military pretensions, evangelical in its worship of property," added Lewis H. Lapham.[76] And, as if to bring about something of a closure on the issue, the man who has come to symbolize the Democratic Party's idealistic, but also politically vulnerable, opposition to the War in Vietnam, George McGovern, wrote a book in 2004 opposing the policies of George W. Bush, all the while upholding eighteenth-century politicians as models of liberalism at its best.[77]

Anti-Federalist and republican at heart, the Iraq War's leftist critics not only had little sympathy for the rebuilding of Iraq, their polemics offered few suggestions about how they would construct a political system at home appropriate for twenty-first-century realities if their models of political wisdom were Jefferson and Paine. No wonder that some of them began to use language indistinguishable from conservatives such as Robert Bork. "The regime's goal," as Mark Crispin Miller put it, using the kind of vocabulary one associates with those writing for *First Things*, "is to abort American democracy, and to impose on the United States another kind of government entirely."[78] It is as if all friends of the eighteenth century have to hang together, whatever the ideological differences that divide them.

So unexpected was the resistance in Iraq, and so vulnerable was the Bush administration to criticism because of its failure to anticipate it, that leftists were free to attack the war without specifying how and why they would have done things differently. But the issue cannot be ducked forever. The question facing liberals and leftists is whether their criticisms of Mr. Bush's intervention abroad will be sustained if and when, a Democrat finds himself deploying troops somewhere around the world in response to a threat to American values.

A suggestive indication of the future that lies ahead can be found in the fact that some writers on the left, despite a widespread determination to defeat George W. Bush in 2004, were not as willing as others to express their doubts about the militarism and aggressive intentions of the Democratic candidate chosen to take him on. John F. Kerry, from their point of view, was not unlike the hawkish John F. Kennedy. Kerry, after all, voted for the initial resolution to go to war in Iraq, however much he may have criticized the war during the campaign. Like any successful politician, he had ties to wealthy campaign contributors, including military contractors, and could be expected to do their bidding. Nothing in Kerry's record, to his critics from the left, indicated that he shared the suspicion toward military intervention that guides those who protect against globalism and believe that imperialism is America's destiny; on the contrary, as one leftist critic of Kerry and his foreign policy advisors puts it, their plan for the world "diverges from that of the Republicans. But it also endorses many of the [Bush] administration's hard-line policies and in some cases is prepared to go further."[79] There is no denying the fact that among liberal and leftist voters, the strident antiwar language of Howard Dean won significant support during the 2004 primaries and could emerge again as a force within the Democratic Party.

Even if they do not win the presidency anytime soon, Democrats will still be represented in Congress and in the think tanks that develop ideas and position papers, and we could, and should, expect that they will spend considerable time developing a foreign policy profile for their party. With failed states and nuclear proliferation still enormously important issues, Democrats, whether in power or not, will therefore have to take positions on questions that involve the possible use of American military force abroad. When Republicans deploy troops abroad, Democrats, or at least those ambitious enough to harbor presidential dreams, typically support them. When Democrats opt for the use of American troops, they generally face fierce opposition, not only from Republicans, but from liberals still scarred by the experience in Vietnam. To both, a Democrat would have to make the case that, because of the nature of the world in which we live, the United States cannot rule the world on its own, but nor can it pretend that there are no dangerous regimes intent on destroying all the things Americans hold dear. Democrats were once able to do precisely that; especially during the early days of the Cold War when, in fact, they did it better than Republicans. Whether they will be able to do it again is difficult to say, but that they will need to do it again if they are to once again make a case for American greatness cannot be doubted.

〇— Conservatives dominate American politics. Conservative ideas, however, do not. In fact, conservatives have risen to power only by borrowing their ideas from liberals. In the 1930s, conservatives attacked the New Deal, including that radical innovation called Social Security; today conservatives insist that they want to privatize Social Security only to save it. In the 1940s, conservatives opposed American entry into World War II; now they attack Democrats for being soft on defense. In the 1950s, conservatives found no fault with a society in which women stayed home and raised children while men worked; these days, they compete for the votes of working women. Conservatives voted against the Civil Rights Act of 1964, to which now, in their opposition to affirmative action, they swear fidelity. The environmental gains achieved during the 1970s cannot be rolled back unless conservatives stand in front of trees and canyons and proclaim their love of nature. Look at who holds office in America, and you would think that the right governs the country. Pay attention to what they say—but not, of course, to what they do—and you would be convinced that liberalism had triumphed.

The oddest aspect of liberalism's retreat from greatness is that liberals have so much of which they can be proud. Without liberalism, supporters of states' rights and property rights would have triumphed over ideals of civil rights. Take away the New Deal and the Great Society, and that many more Americans would be living today in conditions no twentieth-century human being could accept. Had liberals not been willing to challenge totalitarianism, and to bring about the changes in fiscal policy and governmental structure necessary to do so effectively, who can say how many people in the world today would be denied basic freedoms? No wonder conservatives appeal to liberal ideas; their own, at least in their original form, ought to make them ashamed. It is true that liberals have overreached from time to time, legislating equality too bluntly or regulating business too enthusiastically. Conservatives rightly called them on their excesses, not, as it turns out, to replace liberalism, but to adjust its sights more realistically. In these seemingly more conservative times, a book like Louis Hartz's *The Liberal Tradition in America*, which saw liberalism victorious everywhere, would seem out of date; actually, its thesis has never been proven more relevant.[80]

Liberalism won the battle of ideas for one simple reason: the twenty-first century comes after the eighteenth. The aristocratic order that conservatism defended in Europe—and to a lesser degree in the American South—is gone for good, and no one argues that it ought to make a comeback. Equality is so powerfully hardwired into American political culture that the only way conservatives can further inequality is by claiming to speak in the name of the people against the arrogance of the elites.[81] For better or worse, liberty in contemporary times is defined as not only the right of businessmen to get what they want, but the right of everybody else to get what they want as well. These are the brute facts of contemporary American political life. No one can argue against them. Yet liberals, who for the past century or so have worked these facts to their advantage, have, in the past few decades, sat back and allowed conservatives, whose most cherished ideals stand in radical discord with the real world around them, to beat them at their own game.

If conservatism in America is all energy and no ideas, liberalism is all ideas and no energy. The problem liberals face is not a paucity of compelling rationales; health insurance is as needed today as it was when proposed by Harry Truman in 1948, the free market continues to make a mess of industries as important to American well-being as energy and transportation; twenty more years of Republican environmental policies and there won't be much of an environment left to protect; and government, as Republicans prove in deeds if not in words, is far more often the people's friend than their enemy.[82] The problem liberals face is that they are convinced that their ideas are unloved, so unloved, in fact, that they can only be achieved if disguised in conservative clothing. About this, contemporary liberals may, for the foreseeable future, be correct; the American mood, as the Republican victory in the 2004 presidential election demonstrated, is not only more conservative than it once was, but as wary and suspicious of government as ever, not the best environment in which to trumpet programs that would be as costly as they would be far-reaching. But at the very least liberals ought to be able to overcome their perpetual sense that the country they have generally governed well is somehow not really their country.

There once did exist a form of conservatism that stood for American greatness, associated with such leaders as Hamilton, Marshall, Webster, and Lincoln. But the causes for which those eighteenth- and nineteenth-century conservatives fought—a strong central government, national citizenship, equal rights— shifted over the course of the twentieth century to liberals, just as the more radical agenda of the anti-Federalists and Jeffersonians eventually constituted the core ideas of conservatism. Since that shift took place—roughly during the 1920s and the 1930s—there has never been a conservative idea that has taken root, flourished, and, as a result, made America a better place. Every innovation that Americans take for granted today, from a government that offers them security to the chance to own their own home and send their children to college, was supported by one of America's more liberal ideology and opposed by its more conservative one. Thus are the fates of American greatness and American liberalism inextricably tied; we will be experiencing little of the former unless the latter can revisit its flirtations with smallness and decide that, in opting for the good over the great, the small over the big, the local over the national, and the particular over the universal, it took the wrong course.

V Great Once More?

The ideal political system should consist of a conservative party modeled on the British Tories under Benjamin Disraeli and a liberal one based on the social democratic idea brought to fruition in postwar Europe. The reason America has retreated so far from greatness is because its political system currently contains neither.

There did exist at one time a Republican Party that tried to act as the conscience of the nation in a way not dissimilar from nineteenth-century Toryism. For lack of a better term, that tradition, with its origins in Theodore Roosevelt's presidency, came to be called liberal Republicanism since its last great representatives, Nelson Rockefeller and John Lindsay, were, when it came to government, big spenders. But liberal is not quite the right adjective to describe this political tendency; the writer Geoffrey Kabaservice is closer to the mark when he characterizes members of the East Coast establishment as "guardians."[1]

Patrician guardians such as Kingman Brewster and Elliott Richardson served as trustees for so many organizations because trusteeship embodied the principle of disinterestedness. Taking a long view of society, the guardians sought to protect the nation—its history, its natural environment, its institutions, its ideals—

against those tempted to use political power to line their own pockets or to reenforce their privileges. Dispassionate to their core, the guaradians were ill prepared for, and could not survive, the passions of either the New Left or the emerging conservative right. The fact that the last president to embody their patrician heritage shares the same name as the first president to ignore them without shedding a tear gives the story of their demise an oedipal dimension, but even if the younger George Bush had not repudiated the policies of his father, guardian-style politics were doomed in America's current atmosphere of populistic resentment and expectations for immediate results.

Just as doomed were liberal parties that presumed to speak on behalf of the idea of one nation. Throughout the twentieth century, parties of the left typically based themselves on labor movements, hardly a formula for embodying national solidarity since labor exists in an eternal conflict with business and is quite capable of putting its own needs before those of the rest of society. Still, working people have usually been among the largest of all potential interest groups, making at least plausible the claim, as William Beveridge put it in his famous report presented to the British Parliament in 1942, that social insurance would create "a sense of national unity overriding the interests of any class or section."[2]

Striving for the universality such a formulation implied, social democratic and labor parties in Europe advocated policies meant to apply to all, an approach to public policy that Franklin Delano Roosevelt adopted with the development of Social Security during the 1930s. The United States never followed up on the New Deal by developing a classic European social democratic welfare state; when we eventually addressed policies involving health insurance for the elderly and the poor, we relied to an unusual degree on private rather than public solutions.[3] Yet we still aimed for a Great Society rather than a good enough one. Now even a good enough society seems beyond our reach. Domestic programs either failed to solve the problem for which they were addressed or succeeded beyond anyone's expectations. In both cases they lost public support, either because voters viewed them as wasting money or because they created hordes of new middle-class citizens who resented seeing their taxes spent on people poorer than themselves. Convincing middle-class Americans that they are better served by what government can do for them than they are punished by what government takes from them is as difficult a political task as one can define, yet it is an essential one to carry out if the Democrats are ever again to be a forward-looking and optimistic political party.

America's two greatness-oriented political tendencies imploded at roughly the same time: Rockefeller Republicanism proved unable to stem the Goldwater tide that first emerged in 1964, and Kennedy-Johnson-Humphrey liberalism fell into ruin in the streets of Chicago during the Democratic Party convention in 1968. The years since—from Richard Nixon until the George W. Bush presidency and perhaps after—are not ones in which ideas of American greatness have flourished; keeping the republic intact throughout this period seems accomplishment enough, let alone trying to make it stronger. This is an era sandwiched between two of the worst political crises in our history: Watergate, which led to the resignation of a president under threat of impeachment, and the secrecy and distortions characteristic of the George W. Bush administration—worse than Watergate in the view of someone who ought to know[4]—which have further polarized the country and undermined trust in America's political institutions. Along the way were the presidencies of Jimmy Carter and Gerald Ford, names almost synonymous with mediocre performance, and Ronald Reagan and Bill Clinton, both viewed by their supporters with misty-eyed nostalgia, yet neither of whom is ever likely to be remembered for transformative accomplishments. (That Ronald Reagan's death brought with it so many encomiums for a man so disengaged and so frequently unable to distinguish between reality and fantasy suggests how far the greatness bar has been lowered when it comes to presidential expectations.) An entire lifetime can pass—my adult lifetime, actually—without the existence of a single president both willing and able to leave the United States a greater nation after he left office than he found it upon assuming his position. American greatness—always the exception rather than the rule—has been off the agenda of politics for long periods throughout American history, including the Democratic dominance before the Civil War, Republican hegemony during the Gilded Age, and the three administrations prior to the New Deal. It is difficult to say whether the present period constitutes the rival of, or surpasses in its sheer irrelevance, the times of lethargy that preceded it.

In the absence of leadership, American politics currently offers all too few opportunities for American pride. No one, conservative or liberal, can seriously uphold public apathy, opposition research, shakedown campaign financing, symbolic gestures, half-hearted solutions, deliberate distortions, and out-of-control gerrymandering as examplars of democracy at its best. Partisanship tops partriotism in the priorities of most politicians, as candidates spend far more energy knocking their opponents down than building their country up. Americans rush to buy books about the Founding Fathers, thereby passing silent judgment on the mediocrity of their successors. The accomplishments of the greatest generation are exaggerated because the achievements of the present generation are so meagre. As ever, Americans are patriotic to their core and respond positively when leaders evoke the ideals for which they stand. But there is, not far beneath the surface, a defensiveness behind the assertions, as well as in the way they are receieved, as if both leaders and ordinary Americans are quite aware that their political system is failing to bring out the best in them and their country.

With little sense of excitement or expectation of achievement, contemporary American political campaigns, deprived of real issues that can make an actual difference in the lives of citizens, fan the flames of a culture-war not many Americans really want to fight. Instead of uniting around a common purpose, we consider ourselves at odds even when, on issues from abortion to affirmative action, our divisions are not all that deep—certainly not as deep as those that led to the Civil War of the nineteenth century or the domestic unrest of the 1960s and 1970s. We have managed to take the relatively uncontroversial idea of using stem cells to fight debilitating diseases and have turned it into a culture-war football. Our religion, praised by a founder such as John Jay for unifying us, is treated by our candidates as one more way to divide us. No greater acknowledgement of the retreat from American greatness exists than this futile, paralyzing, divisive and—above all else—unnecesssary culture war. It is astonishing that Americans could have been treating each other as enemies during the same period when terrorists decided that all Americans, whatever their political views, religious beliefs, or sexual orientations, were deserving of death. But it defies astonishment that in 2004 the question of gay marriage, as important as that question may be, played a more decisive role in deciding the election than the utterly destructive war in Iraq and the dreadful economic performance of the first four years of the Bush administration.

To overcome the culture wars and return to the business of achieving something for which Americans can be proud, the United States, which ought to have two political parties committed to strengthening the nation, could nonetheless experience significant progress if it only had one. If so, then the immediate political question is whether such a party would be more likely to emerge from the conservative or the liberal side of the political spectrum. Conservatives would have advantages were they to undertake this task. The first to speak seriously in recent years of national greatness were conservatives such as William Kristol. There is, moreover, considerable truth to the conservative claim that liberals became more devoted to rewarding the interest groups that composed the Democratic Party, such as teachers' unions or trial lawyers, than to sponsoring ambitious programs of domestic reform. In the area of foreign policy, the instincts of liberals really did turn isolationist in the wake of Vietnam; for all the appropriate criticisms that Democrats have made of the failure of the Bush administration to anticipate September 11, it is difficult to imagine that a Democratic president would have taken the steps necessary to prepare more adequately for a terrorist attack given the costs involved and the restrictions of civil liberty that might have been necessary. And the tradition of moderate Republicanism is not completely dead; it lives on to some degree in the administrations of Arnold Schwarzenegger in California and Mitt Romney in Massachusetts. In the summer of 2004, one of the intellectuals closest to conservative efforts to adopt the mantle of national greatness, David Brooks, wrote an article advocating that the Republican Party should reinvent itself as a movement in favor of active government, as if to make the case that the party with which he identifies is best prepared to meet the modern world on its own terms.[5]

Yet the energy that has propelled the Republican Party to its current position is too extremist, too angry, too negative, and too polarizing to offer the kind of programs that could unify Americans around common ideals of greatness. In the form it has taken in America, conservatism is an insurgency, not a responsible governing party. The very attributes that make it attractive to voters—moral certainty, distrust of government, suspicion toward others—render it unable to deal with real-world complexities. At least since Edmund Burke, conservatism has insisted that democracy at its worst requires demagoguery at its best; the presence of majoritarianism combined with the absence of wisdom would lead politicians to appeal to the basest of motives and least attractive of emotions. American conservatism has now adopted as the criterion of political success the nightmare against which European conservatism once defined itself. Knowing how unpopular would be its objectives of rewarding the rich and protecting the powerful if honestly acknowledged, it misrepresents its goals and distorts its opposition—all in the name of winning popular majorities. Debate will continue for some time about whether George W. Bush is a genuine conservative, for, in contrast to ideological dogma, he did expand governmental programs (even while failing to find ways to pay for them). But there is no denying that the Bush administration, like the Reagan administration that preceded it, exposes conservatism's major problem in American political culture: it can be true to its principles or electable, but not both at the same time.

Liberals these days are not in a good position to take advantage of conservatism's limitations. True, liberals showed a surprising unity in 2004, so anxious were they to administer a political defeat to George W. Bush. But not only did they fail, they were as unable to mobilize their supporters and to hold their coalition together as the even more highly mobilized conservatives. And having lost in 2004, liberals are likely to find themselves in even worse shape, unable to summon once again a call to arms that would enable them to deal effectively with the string of late-twentieth-century failures that caused Americans to distrust them. The situation facing liberals in the United States is not hopeless; the American political system has gone through one cycle after another as it contemplates the relative merits of relying on the free market or seeking greater stability through government, and the public may eventually tire of the current radicalism of the Republican Party and begin to seek an alternative. But even if liberals were to return to public favor, they would have a dilemma of their own: they would have to satisfy the demands of the interest groups that support their cause, overcome the hostility between more centrist and more leftist forces, and tutor their followers on the need for global leadership. It will take years before liberalism is once again credible in America and even more years before liberals will be able to use that credibility to restore a sense of ambitious national purpose to the United States.

Yet for all its flaws—and they are considerable—liberalism remains more in touch with the universalism that characterized its programs a generation or two ago than conservatism has preserved its links to a tradition of guardian responsibility for the nation. If there is to be a revival of American greatness, it is less likely to come from neoconservatives trying to swing the Republican Party back to the days of Theodore Roosevelt than it is from Democrats reminding Americans of the heritage of Franklin Roosevelt. This does not mean merely copying the New Deal while applying it to contemporary circumstances. Conservatives have made all too effective criticisms of postwar liberalism to which liberals will have to respond; to restore American greatness liberals must avoid triumphalism and accustom themselves, however uncomfortably, to humility. But America greatness does mean taking the idea of common citizenship seriously, an idea that conservatives have all but abandoned, leaving liberals, by default, as the more responsible of America's two dominant ideological tendencies.

What would it take to stop the downward spiral of American politics? As satisifying as it might be as an intellectual enterprise to lay out a full-scale plan for the achievement of American greatness—the kind of thing that Alexander Hamilton did in his

"Report on Manufacturers" and numerous other state papers—the United States is in no mood to take any on anything that would either cost significant amounts of money or disturb our current proclivity for ideological polarization. At the same time, resigning oneself to more of the same trivialization that has characterized our politics since the 1980s is a depressing exercise for anyone convinced that the United States can do better by its own citizens and stand higher in the eyes of the world. One can at least, therefore, ask what kinds of domestic policies are possible in the current environment that would strengthen Americans and, in so doing, strengthen their country. One can also consider the fairly absymal state of citizenship in the United States, at least as measured by voter turnout and citizen knowledge, and ask whether steps can be taken to help Americans live up to the responsibilities membership in a great society entails. And finally the failed War in Iraq, as well as the ever present danger of terrorism, raises the question of whether ways can be found to uphold, and even to further, the values of liberty and equality abroad in which Americans place so much faith at home. There will be no easy path back to American greatness because achieving American greatness has never been easy. But during a time when American military power is so superior to that of any potential rival, it is reasonable to ask whether American nonmilitary power can stand for something more than cynicism, negativity, and futility, one more frustrating of American national purpose than the other.

⌐ Sixty or so years ago, liberals would not have had a difficult time figuring out the appropriate domestic agenda to support a program of national greatness. For policy-oriented intellectuals such as Great Britain's William Beveridge, Gunnar and

Alva Myrdal in Sweden, or the assorted "brain trusters" who gathered together during the New Deal, no society could be considered great unless it maximized the potential of all its citizens. Unfettered free markets, from this point of view, were incapable of such maximization; citizens who were too poor, too ill, too frail—already abandoned by business in its quest for efficiency—would be lost to the nation as well unless the state stepped in to offer them help. Full employment, national health insurance, generous old-age pensions, regulated business, massive modernization projects such as the Tennessee Valley Authority—this was the stuff of national-greatness. As regrettable as the Great Depression and World War II may have been, intellectuals and policy makers of this persuasion believed, at least those events made it clear that never again would society turn back to the inequalities and instabilities of capitalism's laissez-faire youth.

How foreign the domestic ambitions of a previous generation of national-greatness liberals seem against the backdrop of contemporary politics. Laissez-faire not only made its comeback in the Thatcher-Reagan years; all forms of planning, from the brutally inefficient Soviet type to the more benign, but nonetheless cumbersome, version adopted in Western Europe, are on the defensive. The era of big government was over everywhere long before Bill Clinton proclaimed its demise in his 1996 State of the Union message. For anyone contemplating domestic reform capable of dealing with crises both expected and unexpected, these are hardly the best of times. To cite the most conspicuous example, it is no secret that the baby boom generation will soon face retirement, placing historically unprecedented demands upon the ability and willingness of younger generations to support them in their old age. Yet not only are our political institutions unable to take the problem seriously, they are taking steps now, such as tax cuts, that are bound to make the inevitable fiscal catastrophe worse.[6] And the looming problem of the aging of the baby boom generation is a predictable phenomenon, based on knowable demographic facts that no serious experts dispute. When paralysis exists on a problem that can be recognized, the inability of American society to respond to the unanticipated—the potential of a serious economic downturn with considerable unemployment, for example, or a new round of inflation that would punish those on fixed incomes—becomes all that much greater.

Bill Clinton's proclamation on the end of big government came in the wake of his failure to persuade Congress to adopt a system of national health insurance that would have filled one of the huge gaps in the American welfare state. Having watched his ambitious effort go down to ignominious defeat, Clinton could not imagine himself, or any other Democrat, ever tackling big issues the way they had done in the past; no wonder he began to talk about school uniforms and V-chips. But nor are the Republicans likely to address the issue. Unlike Clinton, who failed to move the Congress, George W. Bush did get legislative approval for prescription drug coverage for the elderly. His experience demonstrates that success can be more despairing than failure. To tailor this domestic reform to the needs of private industry, Bush's policy removed one of the most important aspects of the failed Clinton policy: the bargaining power of government to keep drug prices under control. So complex did the legislation become, at least in part because there were so many payoffs necessary to fashion support, that many seniors, fearful of its implications, refused to take advantage of drug discounts and did not express much gratitude to the president, and his political party, for support-ing the law. Serious reform in the area of health coverage is unlikely to come from either political party for some time.

Even though the American political environment cannot support a William Beveridge–style domestic policy, the linkage between the health of citizens and the strength of the nation that Beveridge developed in his report exists as much in 2004 as it did in 1942. Some 40 million Americans are without health insurance. The fact that their diseases may remain untreated—or that, to obtain treatment, they have no choice but to sacrifice some other human need—effectively diminishes the sum total of human accomplishment available to the society in which they live. No nation can be strong when, due to no fault of their own, such a high number of its citizens are rendered weak. A great America should be able to do at least something when inequalities in health care coverage are so dramatic. If it instead concludes that gridlock and fiscal pressure make it impossible to do anything, or that there really is no problem here that cannot be taken care of by the market (as if the market did not create the problem in the first place), then it has chosen other goals than greatness for its future.

A glimmer of hope, though, exists in the fact that political gridlock and fiscal restraint do not exist in some state of nature but are relative to the times in which people live. As the writer Matthew Miller points out, even the most expensive of the domestic policy proposals coming from the left end of the Democratic Party would cost less money and require less of a role for government than many of the initatives advanced by Richard Nixon when he was president. Miller's way of thinking about domestic reform—he calls it, for reasons that will become obvious momentarily, the "two percent" solution—offers a way of thinking about health care coverage that avoids the twin traps of being so ambitious that it is unlikely to win support and too transparently obvious a give-away to private companies that would never permit it to deliver on its promises to ordinary Americans.

In societies with stronger commitments to government than the United States, such as Great Britain and Canada, universality of heath care coverage is still considered an important national objective. These societies have adopted what is usually called the "single-payer" model of health care provision. Government provides health insurance for all. Private insurance is, in Canada for example, forbidden from entering the market. The result is a system that guarantees the same rough level of health care provision to everyone.

Single-payer models have had their advocates in the United States, such as Congressman Jim McDermott (D-Wash). But, as Miller writes, "as a matter of politics, it's not going to happen." Not only that, Miller continues, "It *shouldn't* happen. A system that relies this intrusively on centralized government control of medical prices, medical patterns, and service delivery is not the right model for a sector that will experience an explosion of beneficial innovation in the next thirty years." Just because government-reliant reforms are, and should be, off the table, however, does not mean that the problem of the uninsured must remain unaddressed. Miller offers the outline of a plan that would allow a role for private insurance, upon which conservatives insist, in return for universality of access, a key liberal concept. Such a program would be expensive, but Miller takes great pains to show how a willingess to permit government to spend the same proportion of Gross Domestic

Product that it spent during the Reagan presidency (22 percent compared to our present 20 percent, hence the title of Miller's book) would allow considerable room for a program that would guarantee at least some health care coverage to everyone.

Relying on market-based solutions such as vouchers, conceding significant chunks of the public policy landscape to private corporations in order to win Republican support, and reigning in costs in advance to accommodate stringent budgetary realities hardly seems like a formula for revitalizing American greatness. And in the wake of the arm twisting and double-dealing that went on to secure approval of Mr. Bush's prescription-drug-coverage plan, the bipartisan trust necessary for a solution along Miller's line may not exist for some time. Still, Miller's proposal does have one significant advantage; it establishes in theory, and to a small degree realizes in practice, the point made by Beveridge: to extrapolate from his country to this one, the well-being of all is important not just to Americans but to America. As Miller reminds us, the number of uninsured Americans is equal to the combined population of twenty-three American states. If we think of access to health care as a right, then the number of people without that right begins to approximate the percentage of the American population once denied such basic political rights as the franchise.

Should we think about health care as a right? Franklin Delano Roosevelt did. As legal theorist Cass Sunstein reminds us, Roosevelt, in his 1944 State of the Union Message, proposed a second, or economic, bill of rights, meant to be taken as seriously, at least in FDR's view, as the original Bill of Rights. In that speech Roosevelt made a plea for security, which, he claimed, "means not only physical security which provides safety from attacks by aggressors" but "also economic security, social security, moral security." Americans, the president claimed, should have rights to useful work, sufficient income to provide for their necessities, a decent home and medical care, protection from illness, and other, similar, benefits that would enable them to live in decency. As Sunstein points out, the United States came close to moving in the direction outlined by Roosevelt during the 1960s, but a more conservative U.S. Supreme Court, four of whose judges were appointed by Richard Nixon, stopped any further movement. Nonetheless, economic rights were included in other important documents, including the United Nations Declaration of Human Rights in 1948 and even the interim constitution for Iraq adopted during the period of the American occupation.[7]

While Roosevelt died not long after the speech in which he announced the economic bill of rights, no doubt he would have considered a strong role for government essential to any follow-up. For Sunstein as well, Roosevelt's speech serves as a reminder that no public policy agenda, including laissez-faire, is ever free from the reach of government; if the state supports property rights and allows some to profit greatly, there is no reason why it also cannot support economic rights and allow others their fair share of the national wealth. True of any period, Sunstein's point is particularly true of the present one, during which conservatism has taken the form, not of pure laissez-faire, but of subsidizing private interests with untoward public benefits while denying governmental support to those most in need. When Republicans prove that income can be redistributed upward through public policy, they open up the case for redistributing it downward. By demonstrating the incredible power that government possesses to offer corporate welfare, they make the case for using government to provide for the general welfare.

Still these are more debater's points than they are arguments capable of winning political support for reform. A domestic policy aimed at restoring the conditions of American greatness should link the idea of fundamental economic rights with the kinds of first steps toward their realization outlined by Matthew Miller. Miller himself does precisely that. Having made the case for a bipartisan approach to health care, he suggests that equivalent steps can be taken in other areas of American life. To lead a life of dignity and respect, Americans have a right to a living wage. To advance themselves by taking advantage of opportunities potentially available to them, they need the right to decent schools. Given the reality of global competition, a living wage is not going to come into existence overnight. Considering the dreadful state of American public schools, adequate education for all is a long way off. But conditions for the immediate realization of economic rights were not all that much better when FDR made his speech; by 1944, the domestic reforms of the New Deal were long gone and the eventual postwar resurgence of Republicanism had already begun. Neither the political situation he faced nor his ill-health prevented Roosevelt from outlining what it would take to imagine a society with citizens capable of responding to the challenges facing them, however, and nothing in the present political environment does so either. As with health care, where a single-payer model will not and should not happen, steps to realize other economic rights will not and cannot be based solely upon government. But there remains a craving for them, requiring leadership with more imagination and a greater willingess to spend some political capital than our recent political leaders, of both political parties, have been able to do.

For better or worse, the political and fiscal conditions of the United States force policy makers with ambitious ideas to lower their sights. Considerable doubt exists, though, about whether their sights need to be lowered as much as Bill Clinton did when he turned to former Republican strategist Dick Morris for "triangulation," the domestic political advice that sought to position Clinton midway between conservative Republicans and liberals within his own political party. Bill Clinton's problem was not that he pronounced the era of big government over; it really was, and is. His most conspicuous political failure lay in finding the right language to remind Americans why they have a common stake in one another's fates and in developing more audacious policies to bring that reality into being. Other Democratic politicians may succeed where Clinton failed. But if they do it will be because they will advance at least some conception of what it would mean for American society to treat its own citizens as if their lives really mattered.

⌐ If the American people want to live in a great country, they will have to act as if greatness is something they deserve. At the moment, they do not.

My claim that Americans are not acting as if greatness has been thrust upon them is not meant as a harsh judgment of their moral instincts. In a trilogy of books devoted to exploring how Americans think about the moral and religious issues that have preoccuped philosophers and theologians over the centuries, I found much to praise in our current habits of the heart.[8] Above all else, I concluded, Americans are typically uncomfortable with the culture war that is fought in their name. Moderate in temperament, they distrust extremism of any ideological variety. Tolerant and accepting, their first urge is to reach out, not to stigmatize and exclude. On matters of right and wrong, they distrust absolutes and seek practical solutions to the moral dilemmas they face in their daily lives. For Platonists or religious fundamentalists, the pragmatic dispensation of the moral mind in America can be cause for alarm. For pluralists seeking ways to make democracy work, American morality has real strengths. When it comes to morality, I concluded, Americans think small, an advantage when thinking big leads to violence and war, but a problem when they are forced to address questions of common purpose.

While Americans have moral dispositions that are often admirable, they cannot be characterized as citizens with a zest for politics. Citizens are those who acquire a certain knowledge about the larger world around them, exercise their obligation to vote and keep tabs on those who represent them, seek to give as much weight to the common good as they do to their own self-interest, and work within the instititutions to which they belong to further civic engagement. It is relatively easy to idealize criteria such as these and to find fault with Americans for not living up to them, neglecting, along the way, the fact that they often make sensible judgments about the politicians who compete for their votes.[9] Yet a sufficient body of evidence exists to suggest that Americans have in recent years allowed their conception of what citizenship means to become hollowed out from within.

Among the more mysterious of American political dispositions is the disinclination of so many Americans to exercise
their right to vote. Despite the fact that the United States in
its early years was viewed by so many European visitors as the
democracy for which they were fated, extensions of the suffrage
never came easily to Americans. Considered a privilege long
before it was treated as a right, voting was extended to newer
groups only after passionate campaigns were made on their
behalf, and even then, the idea that one's right to vote could
be taken away if one failed to act as the community expected
remained. Although we tend to think of the extension of the
suffrage as a historical progression, the reality, as historian Alexander Keyssar has demonstrated, is more complex; New Jersey
actually took away the right of women to vote in 1807; America's cumbersome process of requiring voters to register had its
origins in efforts by Protestants to prevent Catholics from voting; and in 1908 New York City attempted to hold registration
on Saturdays and Jewish holidays for obvious reasons.[10] Nonetheless, the forces pressing on behalf of universal suffrage were
irresistible, and while real universality in voting did not come
until very late in American history—court-ordered enforce-
ment of the Voting Rights Act of 1965 did not really begin to
take effect until the mid-1970s—when it came, nearly everyone, with the exception of convicted felons, who wanted to
vote could.

No sooner did Americans win the right to vote than they
began to decide, in worryingly high numbers, that this was a
right they need not exercise. As Thomas Patterson of Harvard's
"Vanishing Voter Project" has pointed out, we would expect
that Americans these days, better educated and more cosmopolitan than their grandparents, would be more likely to vote,

not less. Yet among Americans in general, and among younger Americans in particular, the downturn in voting being experienced in the United States has lasted longer than any previous period of depoliticization in our history and "there is no end clearly in sight."[11] Voter turnout in late nineteenth-century presidential elections averaged 79.2 percent,[12] at least in part because some of those contests, such as the 1896 one between William McKinley and William Jennings Bryan, constituted an example of what political scientist Walter Dean Burnham calls realigning elections that shaped the contours of American politics for a generation or more.[13] (The 1896 turnout was actually slightly lower than the presidential elections immediately preceeding it.) Contemporary elections, by contrast, draw far fewer voters; 49.08 percent of the voting population showed up in 1996 and 51.3 percent in 2000.[14] The 2004 election was a significant exception to this trend of voter disinterest; nearly 120 million people, just below 60 percent of those eligible, came to the polls and, to the surprise of many, the majority of them expressed support for the incumbent rather than voting for the challenger. We cannot know at this point whether 2004 signifies a new trend of upward participation in elections or instead will stand out for its unusual interest. Still, even at 60 percent American participation in elections in contemporary times is below what it has been in the past and one has reason to believe that the stridency of the recent campaign will turn off as many voters in the future as it brought out in 2004.

Seeking explanations for the lack of voter participation, Patterson pays special attention to the kind of politics characteristic of contemporary American elections. The language, for one thing, has been dumbed down. "A computer program designed to assess the reading difficulty of school textbooks found that

Kennedy and Nixon in the 1960 debates used words suited to tenth graders," Patterson points out, "but Bush's and Gore's words in 2000 were pitched to seventh and eighth graders—five levels below the national average."[15] Television journalists search relentlessly for gaffes, leading candidates to avoid spontaneity at all costs, even if the resulting lack of excitement fails to mobilize citizen interest. Constrained by their promises to financial backers not to rock any boats, candidates make promises they cannot possibly deliver, thereby contributing to higher levels of cynicism that further depress turnout. Because of the peculiarities of the electoral college, there is no effective contest in a majority of the states in elections for president, raising for many citizens of those states the question of why they should bother to vote at all. Ideological polarization, charges of voter suppression, and unprecedented sums spent on advertising did not hinder turnout in 2004 but could, if they became more or less permanent features of American politics, alienate potential voters in the future. The American political system was so herky-jerky in its origins and has evolved in so many unexpected ways that no one can properly call it planned. Nonetheless if ever a system seemed designed to discourage voter turnout, it would be ours.

"Low voter turnout is a sign of a content democracy," declared Senator Mitch McConnell, Republican of Kentucky, in 1992.[16] McConnell is widely known for his passionate opposition to campaign finance reform. At least in the short term, his efforts have not been successful; he failed to prevent passage of the McCain-Feingold campaign finance reform of 2002. Still, McConnell does not have much to worry about, since the reforms he opposed were minimal at best, and new ways to work around them will surely be discovered. His seat as safe as as they come, McConnell, although speaking in the language of protecting freedom of speech, has never taken pains to disguise his reasons for opposing campaign finance reform. Awash in funds, large corporate interests and Republican political officeholders can do numerous favors for each other, the former financing a party that needs never-ending streams of cash for its campaigns, the latter sponsoring legislation so beneficial to special interests that it can only pass in the presence of an electorate whose attention span is stunted.

Although far more Democrats than Republicans supported McCain-Feingold, they did so reluctantly, for they, too, were the beneficiaries of a system in which most ordinary Americans pay little attention to politics. Ever since Richard Nixon's victory in 1968, liberals and Democrats have worried that many of the positions they support—civil liberties, abortion rights, reform of the criminal justice system, welfare, affirmative action—did not have majority support and would lose in any kind of direct popularity contest with conservatives. Relying more on courts and administrative agencies to achieve their objectives, they feared that any mobilization of new voters might turn out to favor conservatives determined to carry out the agenda of the religious right. Just as Republicans came to rely on K Street lobbyists, Democrats received funding and support from ideologically motivated liberal interest groups whose financial backing came from wealthy individuals and foundations, not from the accumulated small contributions of millions of members. Although both of America's contemporary parties might gain were citizens to become more active and engaged, both might also lose, and politicians, ever cautious, prefer not to take the risks involved in upsetting a system that works well enough for them, however poorly it works to create a country more powerful than the special interests it contains.

Most advances in greatness occurred in the United States when one segment of the elite, frustrated by the delaying tactics of other powerful interests, turned to the mobilization of voters to realize their agenda. American Whigs, for example, who in 1848 denounced the idea of suffrage extension as "a system of communism unjust and Jacobinial,"[17] eventually realized that suffrage reform was inevitable and supported it. FDR's New Deal coalition worked around the Republican dominance of the 1920s by seeking new voters in the South and in rural America, the very same strategy promoted by a key advisor to Richard Nixon to promote a Republican realignment.[18] "Elites now have fewer incentives to mobilize non-elites, and non-elites have little incentive to join with one another," write political scientists Matthew Crenson and Benjamin Ginsburg, a statement that, despite the obvious exception of 2004, does accurately characterize the general trend of American politics over the past two or three decades. "The two circumstances have operated in combination with one another to produce a new politics of individualized access to government and a new era of 'personal democracy' for those in a position to take advantage of its possibilities." The result, in their opinion, is a transformation from engaged citizens to disengaged ones that rivals in importance, and in some ways caused, the better-known transformation from liberalism to conservatism. "The rightward drift of American politics since the 1970s is, at least in part, a by-product of leftward demobilization," Crenson and Ginsburg conclude. "Today's progressives, unlike their Jeffersonian forebears, seldom seek to advance the interests of the disfavored by enlisting them in grassroots political movements. Today's conservatives, therefore, unlike their Federalist predecessors, are not so driven to compete for popular support as a means of political self-preservation."[19]

When they use the term "personal democracy," Crenson and Ginsburg refer to a society in which institutional restraints have been weakened, enabling those with self-interested agendas to seek to fulfill them directly without having to modify their demands for the sake of coalition building. The most important of such institutions historically have been political parties, which, in the classic textbooks of 1950s political science, were seen as capable of aggregating interests in ways that made majority government possible. As a result primarily of reforms introduced by Democrats to lessen the power of party bosses and to bring about greater democracy from within, parties were increasingly stripped of their ability to discipline candidates and to impose order on their followers. The result is that we lack not only political parties that stand for the idea of one nation, we are missing parties capable of doing more than serving as fund-raising machines, and even that role may become less important for them in the age of internet- based campaigning. Political scientists Marc Landy and Sidney Milkis have argued that one of the reasons we no longer seem to have great presidents is because we no longer have strong political parties; those episodic periods in which greatness flourished throughout American history, such as the era of Abraham Lincoln, were also periods in which parties were built. Now politicians find little use for the parties upon which they relied to get themselves elected; conservatives like Richard Nixon and Ronald Reagan frequently ignored the pleas of other Republican leaders, for example, just as Bill Clinton did with Congressional democrats.[20] Even if a political leader wanted to mobilize citizens in order to break a political stalemate, the institutional vehicle for doing so no longer exists.

Parties are not the only political institutions that have lost their capacity to mobilize citizens. Many of our best-known civic organizations, the kind that represent veterans and the elderly, for example, or those that lobby on behalf of a cause such as civil liberties, have transformed themselves, in Theda Skocpol's words, "from membership activities to professionally managed institutions and advocacy groups." As a result, the mobilization of citizens is as unlikely to take place in civic federations as it is in political parties. "The United States today has the most pluralist polity in the world," Skocpol concludes, "yet associations claiming to speak for the people lack incentives and capacities to mobilize large numbers of ordinary people through direct personal contacts and ongoing involvement in interactive settings."[21] Democracy is increasingly defined by Americans as something that happens on their behalf, not as something in which they take an active part. Content to pay dues rather than attend meetings, they give political organizations remarkable leeway to remove from their own shoulders the difficult and time-consuming process of what used to be called self-government.

This sense of decay from within applies to nearly all American institutions, not just political ones. In their religious lives, Americans are frequently attracted to faiths that emphasize purity of conviction more than they insist on institutional affiliation, a tendency only reenforced in the wake of scandals involving officials in both Protestant and Catholic circles.[22] As we know from the research of Robert Putnam, they do not join organizations and work actively within them to the degree they did in the past.[23] They have been given more than enough reason to put their self-interest before the interests of the corporations for which they work in the wake of the accounting scandals that brought down firms such as Enron. The media has not been able to maintain its reputation for fairness in the wake of its own problem with journalists who plagiarize and television stations that become cheerleaders for political causes. No wonder that when it comes to the most important institution of all, at least for purposes of realizing what holds us together and defines us as a collective identity, Americans express such distrust in government.[24]

As depressing as this scenario of disengagement may seem, however, there is one arena in which the notion of an engaged citizen might reassert itself and, in so doing, help put ideas about American greatness back into circulation. Oddly, for a society that distrusts politics and government so much, institutional renewal may not come from intimate associations like the family before extending itself to more impersonal organizations such as political parties. On the contrary, it is precisely changes in the area of politics, especially partisan politics, that foreshadow potentially important developments in institutions closer to people themselves.

Americans have never really had to pay much of a price for their lack of interest in politics; even though both parties engaged in little citizen mobilization, neither did they set out to take full advantage of the fact that most Americans remain so disengaged. This changed during the George W. Bush administration. While all political leaders dissemble, President Bush took the art to a new level, insisting that tax cuts that put money in the pockets of the rich were designed to serve the needs of middle-class voters and justifying his foreign policy actions, especially the War in Iraq, on claims that turned out not to be true. No matter what the policy area, the administration's combination of secrecy and misrepresentation, too systematic to be written off as a fluke, was designed to take advantage of the fact that ignorance of policy details outside the beltway enables interest groups inside the beltway to get what they want.

This willingness to use unequal access to information to their own advantage extended far beyond matters of legislation. No neutral body presumed to act in the national interest—from the Congressional Budget Office to the scientific review boards—was held free from partisan pressure, and data that did not conform to the administration's ideological convictions was dismissed out of hand, both kinds of actions reenforcing the notion, widely accepted among a cynical electorate, that no one can ever be trusted to represent the common interest. The admistration knew that not only was public opinion unorganized, but journalists, out of a mistaken belief in what objectivity demanded, would treat the administration's claims as one side of a two-sided story rather than as pure partisanship. What to others were sources of concern— distrust of government, ignorance about the world, restrictive voting rules, biased intelligence, gerrymandered districts drawn so precisely that no real reason to vote existed—the administration saw as advantageous. Not even the upsurge in newly mobilized Republican voters in 2004 changed this picture much. As many commentators pointed out, the Democrats in 2004 ran on issues while the Republicans ran on values. Because they were voting on gut feelings rather than on the policy successes or failures of the candidates, these new

Republican voters are unlikely to be transformed into citizens who pay avid attention to national and international politics and cast their votes accordingly.

Yet this attempt to pursue partisan goals by taking advantage of the low level of engagement with politics characteristic of Americans wound up stimulating a new round of political engagement, not that surprisingly, perhaps, given the insistence by conservatives that policies can frequently produce unanticipated consequences. For one thing, President Bush's overt partisanship helped to revive interest in politics, surely a development that anyone who takes politics seriously ought to appreciate. It is highly unlikely that any revitalized parties to emerge from the American political system will resemble the mass membership organizations of old. But by appealing so strongly to the Republican base of strong supporters, Mr. Bush invited Democrats to do the same, and they responded in the 2004 election with a burst of political energy that, while unable to elect their candidate as president, stood in sharp contrast to their relative lethargy in 2000. The size of Mr. Bush's popular majority puts Democrats on the defensive, but their newfound political energy is likely to make itself felt once again as Mr. Bush pursues the radical agenda for his second term to which he has committed himself.

Still it is a long step from the revival of political institutions to the rebirth of all those institutions that will have to be strengthened if the United States is ever again to take the idea of greatness seriously. In the 1960s, leftists talked about a long march through institutions, which meant that they planned to take them over, one by one. Now the task is to march through them to bring them back to life, one by one. American greatness can never be achieved through the uncoordinated actions of indviduals, for it is by its very nature a collective product. But nor can it be achieved from on high, as if government, which can build highways or send people into space, can proclaim a great society into existence by passing the right laws and spending sufficient amounts of money. A great America requires the kinds of intermediate institutions that Americans have not cared about enough to sustain: political parties capable of aggregating and mobilizing citizens; interest groups that crave members and not just contributors; labor unions that seek to create and not only to protect jobs; business firms that invest in those who work for them; and religions that do more than develop clever marketing campaigns to keep members from leaving one church to join another. Entralled with freedom, Americans unshackled themselves from the demands of institutions. Now they may be learning that all important values, including freedom itself, are dependent on institutions for their sustenance.

By itself, institutional revitalization cannot bring a great America into existence. But it is a precondition for everything else; the kind of policy stalemates the United States experiences in areas such as health care are a direct result of the low level of citizenship mobilization, and the latter, in turn, contributes more than its share to the kind of politics that emerges when polarization and legislative impotence dominate the agenda. This is, after all, what one has to expect in a democracy; however important leaders, policies, and programs may be, greatness will not come about unless Americans care enough about it to will it into existence. If they do not take it into their own hands, no one can be expected to do it for them.

⌒— As Samantha Power makes clear in her remarkable book *"A Problem from Hell,"* Bill Clinton was anything but enthusiastic about deploying American troops to stop the unusual number of outbreaks of genocide that had occurred while he was president.[25] Part of the explanation for his hesitancy lay in the furious response he could anticipate from the Republican right for any overseas commitments. The kind of bipartisan cooperation that had existed when Harry Truman proposed the Marshall Plan had been long gone in Washington, and Clinton knew that any costs in American lives would be quickly seized upon by his Republican opponents to further undermine his presidency.

Yet Clinton also understood that any significant foreign policy actions would be unpopular on the left. Every now and then a prominent American leftist would support the case for humanitarian intervention—Power's most striking example involves George McGovern, the symbol of American weakness, who argued passionately for intervention to stop the genocide in Cambodia—but such examples were few and far between. In theory, liberals were opposed to the gross violations of human rights and brutal policies of repression that seemed to be breaking out all over the world during the 1990s, but in practice most of them were content to look the other way.

For at least some American liberals, the two defining events of the George W. Bush presidency, September 11 and the Iraq War, changed the way they thought about America's relationship with the world. For every Susan Sontag or Noam Chomsky, there seemed to be a Michael Ignatieff, Paul Berman, George Packer, Kenneth Pollack, Christopher Hitchens, or contributor to the *New Republic*. Discovering a sense of patriotism they did not know they possessed, they found themselves, in the wake of the terror attack on American soil, hanging American flags from their balcony, conceptualizing Islamic terrorism as a form of totalitarianism that required actions not unlike those of the Marshall Plan and the Cold War, and arguing publicly that the president's decision to retaliate against al-Queda by invading Afghanistan was the right thing to do.[26] In retrospect, September 11, however much it spurred liberals to rethink their assumptions, only contributed to a reexamination that was already under way. For the journey toward their willingness to support American military intervention overseas had already begun in their sense of shame at America's, and Europe's, failure to do more to stop dictators such as Slobodan Milosovic or to prevent tribal slaughter in Rwanda.

Only this sense that the United States had stood back in the face of genocide explains why a surprisingly large number of intellectuals supported President Bush's extension of the war on terror to include the overthrow of Saddam Hussein's regime. None of them could be called admirers of the president's domestic agenda. Nor were they neoconservatives who had worked for years behind the scenes to advocate a new military posture for the United States. Instead they were, to one degree or another, liberals. The United States, they believed, should not and could not be on the wrong side of people calling for democracy and liberty. For too long, American foreign policy had been characterized either by an unrealistic idealism from the left, which avoided military entanglements entirely, or a cold-blooded realpolitik from the right, willing to trade with, and thereby strengthen, dictatorships, espeically including the one in Saudi Arabia that seemed to be too close to terror for comfort. What we need, Michael Ignatieff wrote, is "a viable position between cynicism and perfectionism."[27] The age-old conflict in international relations between idealism and realism has to be resolved in favor of a new combination of both.

If ever there was a justification for war based on liberal premises, the one against Iraq seemed to offer it. Saddam Hussein himself had been encouraged by conservative foreign policy realists for reasons of state during the Iran-Iraq War, proof enough, to a certain kind of liberal, that conservatives could not be fully trusted when it came to fighting on behalf of democratic ideals. His regime had used reprehensible weapons against its own people and, so far as anyone could tell, was prepared to use them again against others. Should the war have proven successful, the task of encouraging democracy in other Middle Eastern autocracies would have been made that much easier. Perhaps in the best of all possible worlds, the invasion should have been led by a broad international coalition supported by a United Nations resolution, but liberal advocates for the war were not wrong when they pointed out that the United Nations was not well equipped to take strong action against dictatorships, given how many dictatorships were members, and that European skeptics of the Iraqi War had also been unwilling to do much about the horrors in Bosnia. For whatever reason, genuine conviction or political cover, a number of America's best known liberal politicians, including John F. Kerry, John Edwards, Richard Gephardt, and Hillary Clinton, voted for the resolution to go to war in Iraq. If there still existed a Vietnam Syndrome, they were no longer paralyzed by it.

"Were we wrong?" asked the editors of the *New Republic* fifteen months after the War in Iraq began, concluding that they in fact were. Kenneth Pollack wrote that even as the war unfolded, he had a sense that the Bush administration was not pursuing its objectives in the right way, including its blithe dismissal of what turned out to be quite accurate estimates of the number of troops that would be required; once it became clear that the administration was prepared to "match Saddam's reckless and delusional behavior with their own,"[28] he wonders how he could have been so wrong about them. For Anne Applebaum, who had written an award-winning history of the Soviet Gulag, the leading officials in the Bush administration were people who had understood the need to confront the Soviet Union, and she fully expected, wrongly, as it turned out, that they would approach fundamentalist Islam as an ideology requiring a broad coalition to defeat it. Her disappointment that they did not follow such a path is palpable: "this is not an administration that actually perceives itself as a part of something greater than the United States," is how she put it.[29] Politicians expressed many of the same kinds of feelings. After the committee he cochaired found that the intelligence leading up the decision to invade Iraq was flawed, Senator Jay Rockefeller announced that, had he known there were no weapons of mass destruction and no connection to al-Qaeda, he would not have voted for the resolution authorizing war. John Kerry, in his campaign for president, explained that having voted to support the president's authority to go to war, he was right to vote against subsequent authorizations given how badly the war was being waged.

The War in Iraq gave liberals an extreme case of foreign policy whiplash; no sooner had they taken the giant step toward support of military intervention abroad than the incompetence and arrogance of the Bush administration led them to question whether this was the right intervention at the right time. These were not the best of conditions, in other words, to rethink what it would take to develop a foreign policy that spoke to ideals of American greatness. From a longer-term point of view, however, the Bush administration's failures in Iraq may turn out to have provided just the ingredients necessary for a serious revival of ideas of American greatness emerging from the liberal end of the political spectrum. The reason is that there is just as likely to emerge an Iraq Syndrome among conservatives as there was a Vietnam Syndrome among liberals.

The neoconservatives who prepared the intellectual turf for the invasion of Iraq had no qualms about relying on military force, but their refusal to supplement it with other forms of power, including the kinds of "soft power" associated with diplomacy, proved fatal to their cause.[30] Because the Bush administration never committed large numbers of troops to Iraq, neoconservatives can argue, as America's generals did during Vietnam, that the military was never given the tools to do the job. But a far more likely conclusion is that major figures in the Bush administration did not want those tools given to them; Iraq, for them, was not only about toppling a dictator, it was also about proving that the United States could intervene at any time and place of its own choosing and in ways that would not require expensive military mobilization. (Convinced that in a unipolar world Americans faced no significant opposition overseas, neoconservatives also understood that there might exist opposition at home if too many lives were lost or if taxes had to be raised to pay for war.) It never seemed to dawn on them that if Iraq was a test case, failure could be just as much an outcome as success, and that if such a failure occurred, it would not only undermine American power, but the theory of American power that accompanied it.

Such a double failure is exactly what took place in Iraq. Whatever the future of that unfortunate country, no one can credibly claim in the second term of the Bush administration that the United States is so powerful in the world that allies have become superfluous. The idea that people in countries we invade will be so thankful for our actions that they will treat us as liberators rather than as occupiers will be laughed off the stage the next time a Defense Department intellectual proposes it. So will the idea that we can rely on high-tech weaponry and, in so doing, hold American casualities to a bare minimum, thereby leaving plenty of other troops available for duty elsewhere. Gone is the confidence that because of superior intelligence, we can determine with some certainty whether a threat exists against which preemptive or preventive action is required. As a result of the Iraq Syndrome, the United States now understands that world opinion matters—the United States is viewed abroad as a nation-state pursuing its own objectives, not as a Wilsonian dispenser of universal morality—and that no country, not even this one, can obtain its objectives through force if it is unwilling to pay the necessary price.

The United States now has two syndromes to overcome, not just one. If it is to get past Vietnam by demonstrating a willingness to engage itself with the world, it will have to be prepared to use its military. But if it is to get past Iraq and to use its military in wise ways, it will have to overcome its propensity to act unilaterally. True, overcoming two syndromes is more difficult than overcoming one. But the benefit, should a way be found past both of them, is that the resulting combination of idealism and realism is precisely what is necessary for restoring conditions of American greatness.

Appropriately enough, one of the more hawkish of the Democratic national security advisors, Zbigniew Brzezinksi, who in turn had become a fervent critic of the way the Bush administration handled the War in Iraq, wrote a book called *The Choice*.[31] Brzezinski's choice is between an America that tries to go alone in the world or one that works with others to form an international community under American leadership. This is not that dissimilar than the choice made by liberals in the immediate postwar years when they opted both to challenge communism ideologically and to do so on the basis of multilateral institutions—a recipe for American greatness that survived decades before crumbling in Vietnam. And it is a lesson likely to be reenforced by the conservative failure in Iraq. President Bush's rejection of international treaties and his unwillingness to share power with Europe will no doubt encourage foreign policy advisors with transatlantic ties to argue more vigorously on behalf of multilateralism, a process aided by the Bush administration's own turn back to Europe when its Iraqi strategy came unglued. If I am correct that isolationism is not dead within the Republican Party, any seeming quagmire in Iraq could lead President Bush to do in his second term what he never did in his first: encourage a withdrawal from that country (perhaps even after launching a renewed attack upon insurgents), all the while claiming that his goal of transforming Iraq into a democracy had been met. Such a scenario would be unlikely to please the neoconservatives, for whom Iraq is just one of the places in the world that require the application of American military force. Isolationism is a greater enemy to the neoconservatives than the Democratic Party: "I will take Bush over Kerry," said William Kristol, the intellectual godfather of national greatness conservatism in the run-up to the 2004 election, "but Kerry over Buchanan or any of the lesser Buchananites on the right."[32] In the late 1940s, a bipartisan foreign policy was created out of fear of communism. Six decades later, it could emerge out of a need to repair the damage done to America's credibility by its own unilaterialism.

Having abandoned the center on foreign policy, the Bush administration has encouraged liberals, along with less zealous conservatives, to return to the tradition of responsible global management they had long since left behind. In so doing, they have made possible a situation in which the reflexive anti-Americanism and fear of globalism that has come to play such a role on the American left since Vietnam could give way to a new willingness to consider American power as a possible force for improvement in the world, yet tempered, because of Iraq, by the realization that force by itself is never enough. Should this occur, it will lack in both the breadth of its audacity and the shrillness of its arrogance the Cold War consensus that sustained presidents from Truman to Kennedy. As far as revitalizing American greatness is concerned, that is not a bad place to start.

⌒— There is no way of knowing whether Democrats will ever revisit their ideas about American greatness. One indication that they might, however, is the fact that the Bush administration's abandonment of the center applies not just to foreign policy but to all the issues that have faced the United States in the years after World War II.

Consider how the radicalism of George W. Bush sheds new light on the choices made by liberal and leftist thinkers in the past two or three decades. President Bush's extremism on the question of the environment could lead to a rejection of uto pian pastoral visions and a new respect for Gifford Pinchot and the progressive tradition of ecological sustainability. His tax cuts, which cripple the capacity of the nation to carry out its business, may help thinkers of the left develop a new respect for the importance of the nation as an agent of equality of citizenship. By fashioning an effective Republican majority and then using it to pass the legislation he favors, President Bush has proven James MacGregor Burns right and Lani Guinier wrong; majority rule is possible and perhaps even desirable given the right kind of leadership, even if one disagrees with the particular majority that happens to be ruling. In his willingness to bend every rule of fairness to achieve his and his party's objectives, Mr. Bush also reminds liberals of the possibility that, despite the worries of neorepublican communitarians, we just might need a "procedural republic" after all; without some kind of Rawlsian position of disinterest, politics really will reward the stronger, as the Bush presidency has demonstrated with almost daily regularity. Mr. Bush's way of governing has put the Democratic Party in the position of overcoming the divisions between its own ideological wings to a degree that would have seemed impossible before Al Gore's loss in 2000.

Whichever party governs the United States in the coming decades will have to choose between goodness and greatness. Both strains in American thought and culture have made their positive contributions—just as both have their dark undersides. Those who have insisted upon goodness have called on Americans to live up to special ideas that, at their best, inspire people throughout the world, even if frequent invocations of American exceptionalism convince Americans that they are immune to the corruptions of power, which, as their adventures in Vietnam and Iraq demonstrate, they are not. Advocates for greatness, by contrast, have been forthright in their realism, willing to talk with honesty and a sense of purpose about the costs that leadership imposes on Americans, even if, in their determination to bring about reform at home and abroad, they have been guilty of overriding domestic hesitations and arrogance in their determination to get the job done. In the best of all possible worlds, the best features of goodness and the best ones of greatness would be linked while their negative sides would be ignored. But that is unlikely to happen, and even if it did occur, it would be likely to produce unanticipated consequences. In the world in which we actually live, goodness and greatness come as fairly complete packages, warts and all, and one has to make a choice between them.

The presidential election of 2004 in this context offered two contrasting styles of leadership from which Americans could make their choice. One, embodied in President Bush's campaign for reelection, made fear central to its appeal, reminding Americans of the dangers that faced them, insisting on its own toughness and competence, and ridiculing its opponents as hopelessly naive and inconsistent. Not much given to offering specifics of the policies he would pursue in a second-term, President Bush campaigned on the basis of his faith in American exceptionalism, his clear conviction that, especially in contrast to Europe, the United States remained a society graced by God with the ability to discern good from evil and, reluctantly but firmly, to assume the burden of making the world a better place in which to live. The events that framed Mr. Bush's presidency, especially the September 11 attack on the United States, were new, but the images, symbols, and language were old. As if by instinct, Mr. Bush combined missionary language of nineteenth-century evangelicals, the honor-first priorities of Andrew Jackson, the suspicious distrust of Andrew Johnson, the political opportunism of Richard Nixon, and the hopeful message of Ronald Reagan into one package, a bringing-up-to-date of all the themes of American goodness that have constituted the fundamental default position of American political culture for more than two centuries.

President Bush's opponent, Senator Kerry, by the very nature of American politics, also presented himself as a tough leader willing to make difficult choices. But the language he used and the messages he sent were more in line with the multilateralist proclivities of Woodrow Wilson, Franklin Delano Roosevelt, and the bipartisan leaders who fashioned America's approach to the Cold War. By speaking of nuance and complexity, Mr. Kerry made himself vulnerable to the charge of flip-flopping, but at the same time he was asking Americans to recognize that the world in which they lived was indeed complex and did indeed require nuance from its leaders. By trying to bring Americans closer to one another, as well as closer to the rest of the world, Senator Kerry attempted to fashion a program around ideas of greatness rather than goodness. The problems he faced in doing so were not entirely of his own making. Greatness has nearly always been on the defensive in American political culture, and it takes a very special kind of leadership, or an unusual combination of circumstances such as a world war or a major depression, to induce Americans to accept its demanding requirements.

Rarely are Americans offered as much of a choice as they were in 2004, but this election gave them an opportunity to ponder not only the differences between liberalism and conservatism—or the different qualities associated with one man who served in Vietnam and another who did not—it also gave them as clear a choice between goodness and greatness as they are ever likely to have. However much intellectuals, politicians, generals, and journalists may urge Americans to go one way or another, in a democracy people themselves get to pick the kind of society they will have. In making their choice in 2004, Americans wrote one more chapter describing the ongoing tension between goodness and greatness that has dominated their history and political culture since the colonists began to consider their independence from Great Britain. By reelecting George W. Bush, despite the egregious failures and procedural radicalism he demonstrated in his first four years, Americans opted to hold fast to the idea that they are a special people blessed by God to do great things, no matter how much the rest of the world views them as prisoners of their own innocence.

It perhaps ought not to come as a surprise that goodness won out over greatness in 2004, for goodness nearly always has had the upper hand in American politics and culture. But even after September 11 both Americans themselves and the others with whom Americans share the globe had the right to expect something else: a growing maturity and self-confidence that would have responded to the terrorism unleashed on that day with a sense of duty to the world's security; a willingness to understand the sacrifices necessary to sustain a position of global responsibility; and an acknowledgment that responding to terrorism involves reaffirming and celebrating liberal values as much as it means preparing for violent conflict. Americans disappointed the world by their choice in 2004. It remains to be seen whether in the future Americans will also come to realize that they disappointed themselves.

ACKNOWLEDGMENTS

One day not that long ago Fred Appel of Princeton University Press came by my office and asked me what I was working on. Lo and behold, we now have a book. Fred's encouragement, advice, and support was indispensable to its completion. He suggested that the Spencer Trask Lectures at Princeton might prove an appropriate venue for these ideas and then encouraged the Committee on Public Lectures to invite me. I am indebted both to him and to the Committee for extending this honor to me.

Richard Wrightman Fox and Robert Wuthnow offered sustained readings of the manuscript and many fine suggestions. At Boston College's Boisi Center, Susan Richard and Tom DeNardo provided important assistance. The American Academy in Berlin provided a fellowship, colleagues, and an appropriate work space to finish the manuscript, and I am indebted to Gary Smith, Paul Stoop, Marie Unger, and others there for their help.

My wife and children sometimes allowed me to pontificate— vent might also be an appropriate verb—at dinner. Thanks, as usual, to them for everything.

Notes

Preface

1. Alan Wolfe, *Whose Keeper?: Social Science and Moral Obligation* (Berkeley and Los Angeles: University of California Press, 1989).

2. Robert Putnam, *Bowling Alone: The Collapse and Revival of American Community* (New York: Simon and Schuster, 2000). Amitai Etzioni, *The New Golden Rule: Community and Morality in a Democratic Society* (New York: Basic Books, 1996).

3. I elaborate on these second thoughts in Alan Wolfe, "Is Civil Society Obsolete?" in E. J. Dionne, ed., *Community Works: The Revival of Civil Society in America* (Washington: Brookings Institution Press, 1998), 17–23.

Chapter I. The Good and the Great

1. William Kristol and Robert Kagan, "Introduction: National Interest and Global Responsibility," in Robert Kagan and William Kristol, eds., *Present Dangers: Crisis and Opportunity in American Foreign and Defense Policy* (San Francisco: Encounter Books, 2002), 22–23.

2. David Frum and Richard Perle, *An End to Evil: How to Win the War on Terror* (New York: Random House, 2003), 119.

3. David E. Sanger, "Making a Case for Mission," *New York Times*, April 14, 2004, 1.

4. Cited in Kathleen Dalton, *Theodore Roosevelt: A Strenuous Life* (New York: Knopf, 2002), 338.

5. George P. Fletcher, *Our Secret Constitution: How Lincoln Redefined American Democracy* (New York: Oxford University Press, 2001), 165.

6. Cited in ibid., 113.

7. Robert Kenneth Faulkner, *The Jurisprudence of John Marshall* (Princeton: Princeton University Press, 1968), 45.

8. 19 U.S. 264 (1821), cited in Daniel Farber, *Lincoln's Constitution* (Chicago: University of Chicago Press, 2003), 54, 57.

9. Cited in Faulkner, *Jurisprudence*, 225.

10. Rogan Kersh, *Dreams of a More Perfect Union* (Ithaca: Cornell University Press, 2001), 267–76.

11. Cited in Morton Keller, *Affairs of State: Public Life in Late Nineteenth-Century America* (Cambridge: Belknap Press of Harvard University Press, 1977), 252–53.

12. Fletcher, *Our Secret Constitution*, 137–38.

13. Walter Russell Mead, *Special Providence: American Foreign Policy and How It Changed the World* (New York and London: Routledge, 2002).

14. Samuel P. Huntington, *The Soldier and the State* (New York: Vintage, 1964), 270–88.

15. Cited in Warren Zimmerman, *First Great Triumph: How Five Americans Made Their Country a World Power* (New York: Farrar, Straus, and Giroux, 2002), 120–21.

16. David M. Kennedy, *Freedom from Fear: The American People in Depression and War, 1929–1945* (New York: Oxford University Press, 1999), 386.

17. John B. Judis, *The Folly of Empire: What George W. Bush Could Learn from Theodore Roosevelt and Woodrow Wilson* (New York: Scribner, 2004), 75.

Chapter II. From Politics to Philosophy

1. Gordon Wood, *The Radicalism of the American Revolution* (New York: Knopf, 1992); Bernard Bailyn, *The Ideological Origins of the American Revolution* (Cambridge: Harvard University Press, 1992).

2. Stanley Elkins and Eric McKitrick, *The Age of Federalism: The Early American Republic, 1788–1800* (New York: Oxford University Press, 1993), 24.

3. David Riesman, with Nathan Glazer and Reuel Denney, *The Lonely Crowd: A Study in the Changing American Character* (New Haven: Yale University Press, 1950).

4. Cited in Jackson Turner Main, *The Antifederalists: Critics of the Constitution, 1781–1788* (Chapel Hill: University of North Carolina Press, 1961), 170–71. The story of Ashfield, Massachusetts, can be found on p. 13.

5. Cited in Keller, *Affairs of State*, 65.

6. Eric L. McKitrick, *Andrew Johnson and Reconstruction*. Chicago: University of Chicago Press, 1960), 87.

7. Michael Kazin, *The Populist Persuasion: An American History,* rev. ed. (Ithaca: Cornell University Press, 1998), 12, 36.

8. Stanley Elkins, Eric McKitrick, and Leo Weinstein, eds., *Men of Little Faith: Selected Writings of Cecelia Kenyon* (Amherst and Boston: University of Massachusetts Press, 2002), 39.

9. Cited in Daniel Walker Howe, *The Political Culture of the American Whigs* (Chicago: University of Chicago Press, 1979), 34; 153–54.

10. Federalist #55, cited in Bernard Bailyn, *To Begin the World Anew: The Genius and Ambiguities of the American Founders* (New York: Knopf, 2003), 124.

11. Cited in Farber, *Lincoln's Constitution*, 200.

12. Herbert Croly, *The Promise of American Life* (Cambridge: Harvard University Press, 1965 [1909]), 170; 173, 207.

13. This ambivalence is perfectly captured in Robert M. Crundun, *Ministers of Reform: The Progressives' Achievement in American Civilization, 1889–1920* (New York: Basic Books, 1982).

14. Michael McGerr, *A Fierce Discontent: The Rise and Fall of the Progressive Movement in America* (New York: Free Press, 2003), 70, 73.

15. Cited in H. Lee Cheek, Jr., *Calhoun and Popular Rule: The Political Theory of the Disquisition* and *Discourse* (Columbia: University of Missouri Press, 2001), 13.

16. McKitrick, *Andrew Johnson*, 89.

17. Cited in Bailyn, *To Begin the World Anew,* 124.

18. Fletcher, *Our Secret Constitution,* 59. See also Daniel Lazare, *The Frozen Republic: How the Constitution Is Paralyzing Democracy* (New York: Harcourt Brace and Company, 1996), 95.

19. Oliver Wendell Holmes, *The Common Law* (Boston: Little Brown, 1881), 1.

20. Louis Menand, *The Metaphysical Club: A Story of Ideas in America* (New York: Farrar, Straus, and Giroux, 2001).

21. Wilfrid E. Rumble, Jr., *American Legal Realism: Skepticism, Reform, and the Judicial Process* (Ithaca: Cornell University Press, 1968), 48–136.

22. Morton J. Horwitz, *The Transformation of American Law, 1870–1960: The Crisis of Legal Orthodoxy* (New York: Oxford University Press, 1992), 213–46.

23. Bruce Ackerman, *We the People, I: Foundations* (Cambridge: Harvard University Press, 1991).

24. David M. Kennedy, *Freedom from Fear: The American People in Depression and War, 1929–1945* (New York: Oxford University Press, 1999), 124, 148.

25. On this point, see Mead, *Special Providence,* 226.

26. Andrew Burstein, *The Passions of Andrew Jackson* (New York: Knopf, 2003), 185.

27. Samuel P. Huntington, *American Politics: The Promise of Disharmony* (Cambridge: Belknap Press of Harvard University Press, 1981), 91.

28. Burstein, *The Passions*, 65.

29. Huntington, *American Politics*, 90.

30. See the discussion in Jonathan Haslam, *No Virtue Like Necessity: Realist Thought in International Relations Since Machiavelli* (New Haven: Yale University Press, 2002).

31. This theme is explored in H. W. Brands, *T. R.: The Last Romantic* (New York: Basic Books, 1997).

32. Cited in Huntington, *American Politics*, 104.

33. Howe, *Political Culture*, 71.

34. Dalton, *Theodore Roosevelt*, 313.

35. Dana Milbank and Jim VandeHei, "From Bush, Unprecedented Negativity," *Washington Post*, May 31, 2004, A1.

Chapter III. Conservatism's Retreat from Greatness

1. Robert H. Bork, *The Tempting of America: The Political Seduction of the Law* (New York: Free Press, 1990), 143.

2. Antonin Scalia, *A Matter of Interpretation: Federal Courts and the Law* (Princeton: Princeton University Press, 1997), 19, 22.

3. Vincent Crapanzano, *Serving the Word: Literalism in America from Pulpit to the Bench* (New York: New Press, 2000).

4. Elizabeth Bumiller, "Bush Vows to Seek Conservative Judges," *New York Times*, March 29, 2002, A24.

5. Bork, *The Tempting of America*, 21–28.

6. Ibid. *Slouching Towards Gomorrah: Modern Liberalism and American Decline* (New York: Regan Books, 1997), 4.

7. Robert H. Bork, "Sanctimony Serving Politics: The Florida fiasco," *The New Criterion Online*, http://www.newcriterion.com/archive/19/mar01/bork.htm.

8. All the quotations in this paragraph come from Robert H. Bork, "Our Judicial Oligarchy," *First Things*, 67 (November 1996), 21–24.

9. *First Things* Editors, "Introduction," *First Things*, 67 (November 1996), 18.

10. "Correspondence," *First Things*, 69 (January 1997), 2–3.

11. Bork, *Slouching Toward Gomorrah*, 334.

12. John C. Calhoun, "A Discourse on the Constitution and Government of the United States," in *A Disquisition on Government and Selections from the Discourse*, C. Gordon Post, ed. (Indianapolis: Bobbs Merrill, 1953), 86, 93.

13. Ibid., 100–104.

14. Ibid., 101.

15. Sanford Levinson, *Constitutional Faith* (Princeton: Princeton University Press, 1988).

16. Harry V. Jaffa, *How to Think about the American Founding* (Durham, N.C.: Carolina Academic Press, 1978), 12.

17. Willmoore Kendall and George W. Carey, *The Basic Symbols of the American Political Tradition* (Baton Rouge: Louisiana State University Press, 1970), 94.

18. Ibid., 21.

19. Cited in John A. Murley, "On the 'Calhounism' of Willmoore Kendall," in John A. Murley and John E. Alvis, eds., *Willmoore Kendall: Maverick of American Conservatives* (Lanham, Md: Lexington Books, 2002), 127.

20. Kendall and Carey, *Basic Squares*, 153.

21. Herman Clarence Nixon, "Whither Southern Economy?" in *Twelve Southerners, I'll Take My Stand: The South and the Agrarian Tradition* (New York: Peter Smith, 1951), 198–99.

22. John P. East, "The Conservatism of Affirmation," in Joseph Scotchie, ed., *The Vision of Richard Weaver* (New Brunswick: Transaction Books, 1995), 164. Willmoore Kendall, "How to Read Richard Weaver: Philosopher of 'We the (Virtuous) People,' " in Nellie D. Kendall, ed., *Willmoore Kendall Contra Mundum* (New Rochelle, 1971), 393, cited in East, "Conservatism," 186.

23. Richard Weaver, *Ideas Have Consequences* (Chicago: University of Chicago Press, 1948), 122–24.

24. M. E. Bradford, *A Better Guide than Reason: Federalists and Anti-Federalists* (New Brunswick: Transaction Publishers, 1994 [1971]), 42, 43, 45, 49, 189; 42.

25. Eugene Genovese, *The Southern Tradition: The Achievement and Limitations of an American Conservatism* (Cambridge: Harvard University Press, 1994), 67.

26. Ibid., *The Southern Front: History and Politics in the Cultural War* (Columbia: University of Missouri Press, 1995), 255.

27. Earl Black and Merle Black, *The Rise of Southern Republicans* (Cambridge: Belknap Press of Harvard University Press, 2002), 4

28. This development is emphasized in Lewis L. Gould, *Grand Old Party: A History of the Republicans* (New York: Random House, 2003), 42–77.

29. Michael Lind, *Made in Texas: George W. Bush and the Southern Takeover of American Politics* (New York: Basic Books, 2003), 82.

30. Richard K. Armey, *The Freedom Revolution: The New Republican House Majority Leader Tells Why Big Government Failed, Why Freedom Works, and How We Will Rebuild America* (Washington: Regnery, 1995), 16.

31. Michael Lind, *Made in Texas: George W. Bush and the Southern Takeover of American Politics* (New York: Perseus Books, 2003), 77.

32. http://www.texasgop.org/library/RPTPlatform2002.pdf

33. *United States v. Lopez*, 514 U. S. 549 (1995).

34. *City of Boerne v. Flores*, 117 S. Ct 2157 (1997).

35. *Printz v. United States*, 117 S. Ct. 2365 (1997);); *Bd. of Trustees of the University of Alabama v. Garrett*, 121 S. Ct. 995 (2001).

36. *United States v. Morrison*, 529 U. S. 598 (2000).

37. *Nevada Department of Human Resources et al. v. Hibbs et al.*, http://www.supremecourtus.gov/opinions/02pdf/01-1368.pdf

38. John T. Noonan, Jr., *Narrowing the Nation's Power: The Supreme Court Sides with the States* (Berkeley and Los Angeles: University of California Press, 2002), 4, 9.

39. Sidney M. Milkis, "Localism, Political Parties, and Civic Virtue," in Martha Derthick, ed., *Dilemmas of Scale in America's Federal Democracy* (New York: Cambridge University Press and Woodrow Wilson Center Press, 1999), 119.

40. *U.S. Term Limits*, 514 U. S. at 846, 849, cited in Farber, *Lincoln's Constitution*, 27.

41. Michael S. Greve, *Real Federalism: Why It Matters, How It Could Happen* (Washington, D.C.: The AEI Press, 1999), 2.

42. David Stockman, *The Triumph of Politics: How the Reagan Revolution Failed* (New York: Harper and Row, 1986), 69.

43. See, for example, Virginia Postrel, *The Future and Its Enemies: The Growing Conflict over Creativity, Enterprise, and Progress* (New York: Free Press, 1998).

44. Grover G. Norquist, M.D., "Elections 2000—The Leave Us Alone vs. the Takings Coalition," http://www.haciendapub.com/norquist.html.

45. Greve, *Real Federalism*, 22–23.

46. Cited in Jonathan Chait, "Manservant," *New Republic*," December 15, 2003, 8.

47. See, for example, David Boaz, "The Bush Betrayal," *Washington Post*, November 30, 2003, B07.

48. Zimmerman, *First Great Triumph*, 340.

49. David Boaz, *Libertarianism: A Primer* (New York: Free Press, 1997), 206.

50. James Brovard, *Terrorism and Tyranny: Trampling Freedom, Justice, and Peace to Rid the World of Evil* (New York: Palgrave, 2003), 289.

51. Charles Murray, *What It Means to Be a Libertarian* (New York: Broadway Books, 1997). Murray does call for limiting veterans' benefits (p. 39).

52. Patrick Buchanan, *A Republic, Not an Empire: Reclaiming America's Destiny* (Washington: Regnery, 1999), 275, 295.

53. Patrick J. Buchanan, *The Great Betrayal: How American Sovereignty and Social Justice Are Being Sacrificed to the Gods of the Global Economy* (Boston: Little Brown, 1999), 17.

54. Michael Kazin, *The Populist Persuasion: An American History,* rev. ed. (Ithaca: Cornell University Press, 1998), 42.

55. Andrew Bacevich, *American Empire: The Realities and Consequences of U.S. Diplomacy* (Cambridge: Harvard University Press, 2002), 23; 29.

56. On the history of this split, see James Mann, *Rise of the Vulcans: The · History of Bush's War Cabinet* (New York: Viking, 2004).

57. Charles W. Colson, "Kingdoms in Conflict," *First Things,* 67 (November 1996).

58. Stanley Hauerwas and William Willimon, *Resident Aliens: A Provocative Christian Assessment of Culture and Ministry for People Who Know That Something Is Wrong* (Nashville: Abingdon Press, 1989).

59. Martin E. Marty, *The Irony of It All, 1893–1919,* vol. I of *Modern American Religion* (Chicago: University of Chicago Press, 1986), 23.

60. Warren L. Vinz, *Pulpit Politics: Faces of American Protestant Nationalism in the Twentieth Century* (Albany: State University of New York Press, 1997), 23–28.

61. Marvin Olasky, *Compassionate Conservatism: What It Is, What It Does, and How It Can Transform America* (New York: Free Press, 2000).

62. Vinz, *Pulpit Politics,* 172, 178.

63. All the citations in this paragraph come from Paul Boyer, *When Time Shall Be No More: Prophetic Belief in Modern American Culture* (Cambridge: Harvard University Press, 1992), 225, 245, 246.

64. For a helpful overview of these ideas and movements, see Alan Jacobs, "Apocalyptic President?" *The Boston Globe,* April 4, 2004, D1.

65. Mark Crispin Miller, *Cruel and Unusual: Bush/Cheney's New World Order* (New York: Norton, 2004), 342.

66. Vinz, *Pulpit Politics,* 172.

67. Ibid., 179.

68. Marc Landy and Sidney M. Milkis, *Presidential Greatness* (Lawrence: University Press of Kansas, 2000).

CHAPTER IV. LIBERALISM'S FEAR OF AMBITION

1. Wills writes about Kendall, his teacher at Yale, in *Confessions of a Conservative* (Garden City, N.Y.: Doubleday, 1979), 17–25. In his writings on Lincoln, Wills, although disagreeing with Kendall's substantive position, argues that he was correct in appreciating the revolutionary implications of the Gettysburg Address. See Garry Wills, *Lincoln at Gettysburg: The Words That Remade America* (New York: Simon and Schuster, 1992), 39.

2. Lani Guinier, *The Tyranny of the Majority: Fundamental Fairness in Representative Democracy* (New York: Free Press, 1994), 17 (italics in original). The article mentioning Calhoun is "The Triumph of Tokenism: The Voting Rights Act and the Theory of Black Electoral Success, *Michigan Law Review* 89 (March 1991), n. 303.

3. Lani Guinier, *Lift Every Voice: Turning a Civil Rights Setback into a New Vision of Social Justice* (New York: Simon and Schuster, 1998), 43–45.

4. John O. McGinnis and Michael B. Rappaport, "Hey Big Spenders: Here's a Law That Could Stop You!" *Wall Street Journal*, February 4, 2004, A16.

5. James MacGregor Burns, *The Deadlock of Democracy: Four-Party Politics in America* (Englewood Cliffs, N.J.: Prentice Hall, 1963), 266, 319.

6. Guinier, *Tyranny of the Majority*, 12, 104, 173, 175.

7. Burns, *Deadlock*, 334–35.

8. For more on this point, see Kevin Mattson's important book, *When America Was Great: The Fighting Faith of Postwar Liberalism* (New York: Routledge, 2004), which came out after my book was set in type.

9. Stanley Elkins, Eric McKintrick, and Leo Weinstein, eds., *Men of Little Faith: Selected Writings of Cecelia Kenyon* (Amherst and Boston: University of Massachusetts Press, 2002), 60.

10. Lynd's masters thesis was published as Staughton Lynd, *Anti-Federalism in Dutchess County, New York: A Study of Democracy and Class Conflict in the Revolutionary Era* (Chicago: Loyola University Press, 1962). See also ibid., *Class Conflict, Slavery, and the United States Constitution* (Westport, Conn: Greenwood Press, 1980 [1967]).

11. Saul Cornell, *The Other Founders: Anti-Federalism and the Dissenting Tradition in America, 1788–1828* (Chapel Hill: University of North Carolina Press, 1999), 2. He cites as examples Kenneth M. Dolbeare and John F. Manley, eds., *The Case Against the Constitution: From the Anti-Federalists to the Present* (Armonk, N.Y.: M. E. Sharpe, 1987) and Jennifer Nedelsky, "Confining Democratic Politics: Anti-Federalists, Federalists, and the Constitution," *Harvard Law Review*, XCVI (1982), 340–60.

12. Saul Cornell, "The Changing Historical Fortunes of the Anti-Federalists," *Northwestern University Law Review*, 84 (1990), 64.

13. Joyce Appleby, *Liberalism and Republicanism in the Historical Imagination* (Cambridge: Harvard University Press, 1992), 23.

14. Michael J. Sandel, *Democracy's Discontent: America in Search of a Public Philosophy* (Cambridge: Harvard University Press, 1996), 138, 162, 164.

15. Ibid., 267.

16. Ibid., 322.

17. Ronald S. Beiner, "Introduction," in Anita L. Allen and Milton C. Regan, Jr., eds., *Debating Democracy's Discontent: Essays on American Politics, Law, and Public Philosophy* (New York: Oxford University Press, 1998), 8.

18. Gary Hart, *Restoration of the Republic: The Jeffersonian Ideal in Twenty-first Century America* (New York: Oxford University Press, 2002), 23, 206–07.

19. Ibid., 236.

20. Christopher Lasch, *The True and Only Heaven: Progress and Its Critics* (New York: Norton, 1991), 29.

21. Ibid., 383.

22. John Kenneth Galbraith, *The Affluent Society* (Boston: Houghton Mifflin, 1958).

23. Ibid., *American Capitalism: The Concept of Countervailing Power* (Boston: Houghton Mifflin, 1952).

24. Juliet Schor, *The Overworked American: The Unexpected Decline of Leisure* (New York: Basic Books, 1991).

25. Ibid., *The Overspent American: Upscaling, Downshifting, and the New Consumer* (New York: Basic Books, 1998), 23.

26. David E. Shi, *The Simple Life: Plain Living and High Thinking in America* (New York: Oxford University Press, 1985).

27. For another account of the politics of consumption, see Lizabeth Cohen, *A Consumer's Republic: The Politics of Mass Consumption in Postwar America* (New York: Knopf, 2003). For Schor's suggestions, see *The Overspent American*, 154, 161.

28. See the responses in Juliet Schor, *Do Americans Shop Too Much?* (Boston: Beacon Press, 2000).

29. Barbara Ehrenreich, *Nickel and Dimed: On (Not) Getting By in America* (New York: Metropolitan Books, 2001).

30. Elkins, McKitrick, and Weinstein, *Men of Little Faith*, 33.

31. E. F. Schumacher, *Small Is Beautiful: Economics As If People Mattered* (New York: Harper and Row, 1975).

32. Bob Pepperman Taylor, *Our Limits Transgressed: Environmental Political Thought in America* (Lawrence: University Press of Kansas, 1992), 22.

33. Henry David Thoreau, "Walking," in *Civil Disobedience and Other Essays* (New York: Dover Publications, 1993), 59, 16–17, 62.

34. For the reference in this paragraph to Pinchot, I am indebted to Taylor, *Limits*, 16–23.

35. Wendell Berry, *Citizenship Papers* (Washington, D.C.: Shoemaker and Hoard, 2003), 10, 159.

36. Bill McKibben, *The End of Nature* (New York: Random House, 1989), 175–76.

37. Ibid., *Enough: Staying Human in an Engineered Age* (New York: Times Books, 2003), 196–97.

38. Taylor, *Limits*, 137.

39. Nader wrote the preface to Schor's essay "Do Americans Shop Too Much?"

40. Ralph Nader, *Crashing the Party: How to Tell the Truth and Still Run for President* (New York: St. Martin's Press, 2002), 18, 314.

41. Senator Al Gore, *Earth in the Balance: Ecology and the Human Spirit* (Boston: Houghton Mifflin, 1992), 161, 220, 226.

42. Bjorn Lomborg, *The Skeptical Environmentalist: Measuring the Real State of the World* (Cambridge: Cambridge University Press, 2001). The author recalls hearing Commoner in the 1970s predict, with great certainty, the exhaustion of oil as a resource by the time this book was published.

43. David W. Noble, *Death of a Nation: American Culture and the End of Exceptionalism* (Minneapolis: University of Minnesota Press, 2002).

44. George Lipsitz, "Foreward," *Death of a Nation*, p. x.

45. I elaborate on these points in Alan Wolfe, "Anti-American Studies: The Difference Between Criticism and Hatred," *New Republic*, February 10, 2003.

46. Jan Radway, "What's in a Name?" in Donald E. Pease and Robyn Wiegman, eds., *The Futures of American Studies* (Durham: Duke University Press, 2002), 59.

47. Keller, *Affairs of State*, 252–53.

48. Ibid., 39.

49. Gary Gerstle, *American Crucible: Race and Nation in the Twentieth Century* (Princeton: Princeton University Press, 2001), 71.

50. Cited in David Hollinger, *Postethnic America: Beyond Multiculturalism* (New York: Basic Books, 1995), 158.

51. Cited in Otis L. Graham, Jr., *Unguarded Gates: A History of America's Immigration Crisis* (Lanham, Md.: Rowman and Littlefield, 2004), 144–46.

52. *New York Times*, March 29, 1984, A16.

53. John F. Kennedy, *A Nation of Immigrants*, Introduction by Robert F. Kennedy (New York: Harper and Row, 1964, 1968).

54. Samuel P. Huntington, *Who Are We?: The Cultural Core of American National Identity* (New York: Simon and Schuster, 2004). My review of the book appeared as Alan Wolfe, "Native Son: Samuel Huntington Defends the Homeland," *Foreign Affairs*, 83 (May/June 2004), 120–25.

55. Graham, *Unguarded Gates*, 16.

56. Vernon M. Briggs, Jr., *Immigration and American Unionism* (Ithaca: Cornell University Press, 2001), 42.

57. David Lowenthal, *George Perkins Marsh: Prophet of Conservation* (Seattle: University of Washington Press, 2000), 158.

58. Edwin Black, *War Against the Weak: Eugenics and America's Campaign to Create a Master Race* (New York: Four Walls/Eight Windows, 2003), 127.

59. Susan Moller Okin, *Is Multiculturalism Bad for Women?* (Princeton: Princeton University Press, 1999).

60. Herbert Gans, "Symbolic Ethnicity: The Future of Ethnic Groups and Cultures in America," *Ethnic and Racial Studies*, 12 (January 1970), 1–20.

61. Stephan Thernstrom, "Rediscovering the Melting Pot—Still Going Strong," in Tamar Jacoby, ed., *Reinventing the Melting Pot: The New Immigrants and What It Means to Be an American* (New York: Perseus Books, 2004), 17.

62. Arthur Schlesinger, Jr., *The Disuniting of America* (New York: Norton, 1992), 121.

63. Michael Walzer, *What It Means to Be an American* (New York: Marsillo, 1992), 35,

64. Will Kymlicka, *Politics in the Vernacular: Nationalism, Multiculturalism, and Citizenship* (New York: Oxford University Press, 1992), 172. See also Charles Taylor, *Multiculturalism and the Politics of Recognition* (Princeton: Princeton University Press, 1994).

65. Huntington, *Who Are We?*, 49.

66. Benedict R. Anderson, *Imagined Communities: Reflections on the Origin and Spread of Nationalism* (London: Verso, 1991), 141–44, 192.

67. Huntington, *Who Are We?*, 22, 61, 137, 294

68. Michael Ignatieff, *Blood and Belonging: Journeys into the New Nationalism* (New York: Farrar, Straus, and Giroux, 1994), 6–7.

69. Hollinger, *Postethnic America*, 13.

70. Carl Ogelsby, "Trapped in a System," in Alexander Bloom and Wine Breines, eds., *"Takin' It to the Streets": A Sixties Reader* (New York: Oxford University Press, 1995), 221.

71. Howard Zinn, *The Twentieth Century: A People's History* (New York: Harper Perennial, 1998), 214.

72. Arthur Schlesinger, Jr., *The Imperial Presidency* (Boston: Houghton Mifflin, 1973).

73. See John Micklethwait and Adrian Wooldridge, *The Right Nation: Conservative Power in America* (New York: Penguin, 2004).

74. Mark Crispin Miller, *Cruel and Unusual: Bush/Cheney's New World Order* (New York: Norton, 2004), vii.

75. T. D. Allman, *Rogue State: America at War with the World* (New York: Nation Books, 2004), 350–51.

76. Lewis H. Lapham, Gag Rule: *On the Suppression of Dissent and the Stifling of Democracy* (New York: Penguin Press, 2004), 133.

77. George McGovern, *The Essential America: Our Founders and the Liberal Tradition* (New York: Simon and Schuster, 2004).

78. Miller, *Cruel and Unusual*, v.

79. Michael Klare, "John Kerry, The Enlightened Hawk," *Le Monde Diplomatique,* July 2004, at http://mondediplo.com/2004/07/02kerry

80. Louis Hartz, *The Liberal Tradition in America: An Interpretation of American Political Thought since the Revolution* (San Diego: Harcourt, Brace, Jovanovich, 1991 [1955]).

81. For an interesting commentary on this phenomenon, see Thomas Frank, *What's the Matter with Kansas?: How Conservatives Won the Heart of America* (New York: Metropolitan Books, 2004).

82. For an effort to address issues such as these, see Ted Halstead, ed., *The Real State of the Union: From the Best Minds in America, Bold Solutions to the Problems Politicians Dare Not Address* (New York: Basic Books, 2004).

CHAPTER V. GREAT ONCE MORE?

1. Geoffrey M. Kabaservice, *The Guardians: Kingman Brewster, His Circle, and the Rise of the Liberal Establishment* (New York: Henry Holt, 2004).

2. William Beveridge, *Social Insurance and Allied Services* (New York: The Macmillan Co, 1942), 172.

3. Jacob Hacker, *The Divided Welfare State* (New Haven: Yale University Press, 20xx).

4. John W. Dean, *Worse than Watergate: The Secret Presidency of George W. Bush* (New York: Little Brown, 2004).

5. David Brooks, "How to Reinvent the G.O.P.," *New York Times Magazine,* August 29, 2004, 32.

6. Lawrence J. Kotlikoff and Scott Burns, *The Coming Generational Storm: What You Need to Know about America's Economic Future* (Cambridge, Mass.: M.I.T. Press, 2004).

7. Cass Sunstein, *The Second Bill of Rights: FDR's Unfinished Revolution and Why We Need It More than Ever* (New York: Basic Books, 2004).

8. Those books are, in order of publication, *One Nation After All: What Americans Really Think about God, Country, Family, Work, Welfare, Family, the Right, the Left, and Each Other* (New York: Viking, 1998); *Moral Freedom: The Search for Virtue in a World of Choice* (New York: Norton, 2001); and *The Transformation of American Religion: How We Actually Live Our Faith* (New York: Free Press, 2003).

9. A thought-provoking defense of citizenship as Americans have practiced it can be found in Michael Schudon's, *The Good Citizen: A History of American Civil Life* (New York: Basic Books, 1998).

10. Alexander Keyssar, *The Right to Vote: The Contested History of Democracy in the United States* (New York: Basic Books, 2000), 54, 65, 157.

11. Thomas E. Patterson, *The Vanishing Voter: Public Involvement in an Age of Uncertainty* (New York: Knopf, 2002), 20.

12. Mark Lawrence Kornbluh, *Why America Stopped Voting: The Decline of Participatory Democracy and the Emergence of Modern American Politics* (New York and London: New York University Press, 2000), 12.

13. Walter Dean Burnham, *Critical Elections and the Mainsprings of American Politics* (New York: W. W. Norton and Co, 1970), 71–90.

14. For 1996, see http://www.fec.gov/pages/96to.htm. For 2000, see http://www.fec.gov/pages/2000turnout/reg&to00.htm.

15. Patterson, *Vanishing Voter*, 41.

16. Keyssar, *Right to Vote*, 314.

17. Ibid., 41.

18. Kevin Phillips, *The Emerging Republican Majority* (New Rochelle, N.Y.: Arlington House, 1969).

19. Matthew A. Crenson and Benjamin Ginsberg, *Downsizing Democracy: How America Sidelined Its Citizens and Privatized Its Public* (Baltimore: Johns Hopkins University Press, 2002), 3; 237.

20. Marc Landy and Sidney M. Milkis, *Presidential Greatness* (Lawrence: University Press of Kansas, 2000).

21. Theda Skocpol, *Diminished Democracy: From Membership to Management in American Civic Life* (Norman: University of Oklahoma Press, 2003), 128, 231.

22. I discuss the anti-institutionalism of American religion in *The Transformation of American Religion*, 37–66.

23. Robert Putnam, *Bowling Alone: The Collapse and Revival of American Community* (New York: Simon and Schuster, 2001).

24. Joseph S. Nye, Jr., Philip D. Zelikow, and David C. King, eds., *Why People Don't Trust Government* (Cambridge: Harvard University Press, 1997).

25. Samantha Power: *"A Problem from Hell": America and the Age of Genocide* (New York: Basic Books, 2002), 326–27.

26. Todd Gitlin, "Blaming America First," *Mother Jones*, January/February 2002, 22ff.; Paul Berman, *Terror and Liberalism* (New York: Norton, 2003).

27. Michael Ignatieff, *The Lesser Evil: Political Ethics in an Age of Terror* (Princeton: Princeton University Press, 2004), 19.

28. Kenneth Pollack, "Mourning After," *New Republic*, June 28, 2004, 23.

29. Anne Applebaum, "Back in the U.S.S.R.," *New Republic*, June 28, 2004, 20.

30. Joseph Nye, *Soft Power: The Means to Success in World Politics* (New York: Public Affairs, 2004).

31. Zbigniew Brzezinski, *The Choice: Global Domination or Global Leadership* (New York: Basic Books, 2004), xi.

32. David D. Kirkpatrick, "Lack of Resolution in Iraq Finds Conservatives Divided," *New York Times*, April 19, 2004, A21.

INDEX